BENCHMARKING STAFF PERFORMANCE

Jac Fitz-enz

BENCHMARKING STAFF PERFORMANCE

How Staff Departments Can Enhance Their Value to the Customer

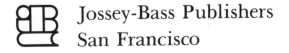

Jossey-Bass Publishers
San Francisco

Substantial discounts on bulk quantities of Jossey-Bass books are available to corporations, professional associations, and other organizations. For details and discount information, contact the special sales department at Jossey-Bass Inc., Publishers. (415) 433-1740; Fax (415) 433-0499.

For sales outside the United States, contact Maxwell Macmillan International Publishing Group, 866 Third Avenue, New York, New York 10022.

Manufactured in the United States of America

The paper used in this book is acid-free and meets the State of California requirements for recycled paper (50 percent recycled waste, including 10 percent postconsumer waste), which are the strictest guidelines for recycled paper currently in use in the United States.

The ink in this book is either soy- or vegetable-based and during the printing process emits fewer than half the volatile organic compounds (VOCs) emitted by petroleum-based ink.

Library of Congress Cataloging-in-Publication Data

Fitz-enz, Jac.
 Benchmarking staff performance : how staff departments can enhance their value to the customer.
  p. cm. — (Jossey-Bass management series)
 Includes bibliographical references and index.
 ISBN 1-55542-573-9 (alk. paper)
 1. Organizational effectiveness. 2. Benchmarking (Management)
 3. Line and staff organization. I. Title. II. Series.
 HD58.9.F58 1993
 658.4'02 — dc20   93-27747
                                                  CIP

FIRST EDITION
HB Printing   10 9 8 7 6 5 4 3 2 1   *Code 9372*

The Jossey-Bass

MANAGEMENT SERIES

Contents

Preface   xi

The Author   xvii

1. Supporting the Business Vision: How to
    Leverage the Hidden Value in Staff
    Departments   1

2. Basic Principles for Successful Benchmarking:
    Avoiding the Activity Trap   26

3. Performance Measurement: Applying Numbers
    in Benchmarking   55

4. Value Planning: Selecting and Launching the
    Right Project   74

5. Data Development: Gathering Useful
    Information   101

6. Evaluation: Developing Strategies for Closing
    Critical Performance Gaps   128

7. Action: Gaining Commitment to Change   150

8. Managing Large-Scale, Multicompany, and
    Multinational Benchmarking Projects   172

9. A National Benchmarking Project: Uncovering
    the True Source of Best Practices   187

    Epilogue   207

    References   211

    Index   213

Preface

This book represents to me another step in the value management journey. For more than fifteen years I have been writing and speaking about measuring value. Since 1986, my company, the Saratoga Institute, has been publishing surveys of the effectiveness of human asset management in corporations. I am often asked why the survey report does not explore topics in greater depth. My answer is that surveys cover a topic in breadth; to achieve in-depth understanding, companies need to benchmark—that is, they need to identify a product or process that is absolutely the best in its class and compare that with their own products or processes to find ways of improving them.

Background and Purpose

The art of benchmarking is still in its infancy. Two years ago, only a handful of people had even heard of it; fewer had done any. In January 1993, I attended a conference on the topic. When one of the speakers asked how many in the audience had been involved in a benchmarking project, fewer than 10 percent raised their hands.

At the time I started writing this book, there were only two or three benchmarking books on the market. Robert Camp's (1989) was the first. He discussed the topic on the basis of his experience at Xerox. Mike Spendolini (1992) followed, reviewing what was being done and amalgamating the different methods into one model. Later, Kathleen Leibfried and Carol J. McNair (1992) described benchmarking, relying on their experiences at Ernst & Young. Each book made a contribution, but all were general descriptions of the methodology of benchmarking. No one has yet focused on applying benchmarking to staff functions or dealt directly with adding value as the driving purpose for benchmarking.

Benchmarking holds a great deal of promise as a means of adding value by helping companies solve major internal problems and exploit key opportunities in the marketplace. The temptation is great, however, to employ benchmarking merely as the latest solution to problems and to involve a large number of people in the activity of benchmarking without having a clear, verifiable business objective.

This book is about adding value to the company through benchmarking staff department processes. Most managers do not recognize the potential value of staff work. They fail to acknowledge that staff actions affect external customer satisfaction by helping to increase internal customer efficiency. In this book, I focus strongly on the point that staff members cannot be equated with expense or overhead. They add tangible value just as line workers do. As organizations search for ways to be more cost effective, they often cut staff, because these people are seen as an expense. When executives begin to understand how to position and manage staff members to add value, they will invest in them in a more positive way.

My final reason for writing this book is to show that benchmarking has more than one face. Spendolini mentioned different levels of benchmarking, and Leibfried and McNair actually gave an example or two, but these writers failed to display the incredibly broad range that is possible with this approach. I have provided two chapters devoted to multicompany and international benchmarking, as well as in-depth examination of national benchmarking of best practices, using a quantitative survey as a starting point. I want to introduce readers to several of the different formulas or models for benchmarking.

Audience

Benchmarking Staff Performance was written for people who are endorsing, managing, or implementing benchmarking projects. The first three chapters should be read by every chief executive who is supporting a continuous improvement program. It will open their eyes to the notion of staff as value adding rather than as overhead or expense functions. This insight will lead them to focus benchmarking projects on adding value to the external customer, thereby giving the company a competitive advantage. It will also help them to focus staff efforts on supporting this goal.

The book should also be read by staff members involved in benchmarking — typically directors, managers, supervisors, and professional employees from functions such as customer service, finance, facilities, human resources, information systems, maintenance, marketing, purchasing, real estate management, research and development, and safety/security. These people are the most susceptible to the unfocused-activity trap. Many companies attempt to implement a new idea or technique without first taking time to fully understand its unique capabilities and limitations. Then mid-level staff members are charged with benchmarking something — anything — to prove that they are on the team. As a result, they often waste time on meaningless applications. By utilizing the value test they will avoid the activity trap.

Organization of the Book

In writing *Benchmarking Staff Performance,* I have attempted to conduct a three-point balancing act: to establish value as the reason for benchmarking, to provide a model for carrying out a typical project, and to illustrate the model with two on-going examples: Typically Ltd. and the Sample Company. I use Typically Ltd. to illustrate and reinforce key points within the text. The Sample Company provides an outlined application of the main model. By following it through the book, the reader may better understand the flow of a standard project.

Chapters One through Three lay the foundation. The first chapter deals with value for the customer as the reason for being in business. I introduce the notion of connecting staff work to customer value, a generally unseen linkage. The chapter also touches on how benchmarking can help add value. Chapter Two outlines the idea, purpose, issues, and applications of benchmarking. Chapter Three illustrates the importance of using metrics or numbers to measure the value of staff processes and other functions. U.S. managers are generally deficient in the ability to use numbers.

Chapters Four through Seven describe the standard benchmarking project, with heavy emphasis on value planning as the starting point. Chapters Eight and Nine are multicompany, national, and multinational case examples drawn from our experiences at the Saratoga Institute. These examples differ somewhat from the standard project and hopefully will open new perspectives on the topic.

General Electric CEO Jack Welch tells us the 1990s are the "Value Decade." He claims that value is based on having a vision, maximizing productivity, and being flexible to change with the market. The epilogue restates the fundamentals of value creation and warns of ineffective quick-fix attempts. It looks ahead at the evolving marketplace and asserts that the winners in the twenty-first century will be those who, while adopting new technology, also keep their eyes on the fundamental issue of adding value. It suggests that activity can be self-satisfying as well as deceptive. The fundamentals of wealth building hinge on distinguishing purpose from activity, understanding the customer's true needs, and building the company's internal capability to serve both the purpose and the customer.

Acknowledgments

The first person I want to acknowledge is my partner and wife, Ellen Kieffer. Without her presence all along the way, this project would have been much more difficult. She not only was tolerant of my preoccupation but also served as a wise sounding board at various points. I appreciate her more every day and can never thank her enough.

The clients who hired us to conduct benchmarking projects deserve my gratitude. We learned together on the earliest projects. The staff at Jossey-Bass, notably the editor of the Jossey-Bass Management Series, Sarah Polster, her assistant, Barbara Hill, and project editor Alice Morrow, were very understanding and helpful. The reviewers of the first draft did a superb job and I have incorporated many of their ideas. The staff of the Saratoga Institute worked without direction during the times when I was deeply involved and needed to devote much attention to completing the manuscript. I appreciate their understanding.

Rod and Helen MacKinlay were helpful in a unique way. Rod is director of Management Information Systems (MIS) Far East for Seagate Technology. He guided me around the issues of leading-edge information technology. Helen and Rod gave me free reign to work at their home in Singapore for a critical week when I was putting the finishing touches on the second draft. John Hetz, former manager of administration at Xerox's Palo Alto Research Center (PARC), provided examples of quantitative measures for a number of administrative functions, along with descriptions of how they were used to add value.

Finally, I want to sincerely thank you, the reader. Your interest in benchmarking staff performance is commendable. Your desire to help your organization and to add value for your customer is essential to your organization's future success. I wish you well and invite you to contact me with questions or to share your experiences. Let us continue to learn together.

Saratoga, California   Jac Fitz-enz
June 1993

To my wonderful friends,
my children: Dan, Kate, Mike, and Peter.
I hope you have learned as much about
life from me as I have learned from you.

The Author

Jac **Fitz-enz** is an internationally acclaimed author, speaker, and consultant. He is recognized as the father of the total-system approach to measuring the return on investment of staff functions. His book *How to Measure Human Resource Management* (1984) set the international standard for quantitative evaluation and reporting of human resource operations. In his latest book, *Human Value Management,* which won the Society for Human Resource Management Book of the Year Award in 1991 as the best human resources publication of 1990, Fitz-enz presented his value management model and provided examples of how excellent companies worldwide are applying it to add value to staff functions.

Fitz-enz is a world authority on the design and implementation of staff strategic management and measurement systems. He has led benchmarking projects and seminars for major organizations worldwide. His methods are currently being applied in more than six hundred companies in the United States and in twenty-five other countries. Clients include Alcan, American Express, Bank of Montreal, Bank of America, Chevron, DuPont, Honda, IBM, Intel, MCI, Merck, National Australia Bank, Prudential, Sears, and Westinghouse.

As president of the Saratoga Institute, Fitz-enz oversees the institute's benchmark network and Best in America programs. He developed its international data network and edits the annual *Human Resource Effectiveness Report* and the *Best Practices Guidebook*. He also writes the *Fitz-enz Forecast,* a quarterly publication that highlights emerging issues, identifies trends, and describes the best practices of leading companies worldwide. Before founding the Saratoga Institute in 1977, he had twenty years of general business experience, including tenure as vice president of human resources functions at Motorola Computer Systems, Imperial Bank, and Wells Fargo Bank.

BENCHMARKING STAFF PERFORMANCE

1

Supporting the Business Vision: How to Leverage the Hidden Value in Staff Departments

Value creation is the ultimate test of any enterprise. There has never been a time in modern commercial history when the creation of value for the customer has been so critical to the success of a business organization. While it has always been a truism that the purpose of every job in every organization at all times is to create value, it is now the code of survival.

The following conversation could have taken place during a staff meeting at the Typically Ltd. Company:

Chief Executive Officer (CEO):   According to the latest quarterly figures, we are continuing to lose market share. What the hell is going on in sales, Charley? Don't your people know how to sell?

Sales Manager: Chief, we can sell all the product we can get. The problem is that manufacturing can't make it fast enough and customer service can't give us up-to-date and accurate account and shipping information.

Production Manager: It's not our fault. Procurement takes forever to get us material. To make matters worse, sometimes they buy too much of one item and not enough of another. The other problem is that human resources takes forever to fill position requests. I've had supervisor and technician positions open as long as eight or nine weeks. If you'd let me do my own hiring I'd fill them in a week. Those are the reasons my plant is running at only 70 percent of capacity. You get us the goods and the bodies and we'll make all the product you can sell.

Customer Service Manager: Charley, we can't give you something we don't have. Accounting takes forever to process account data, so by the time we get them, they're out of date. And the shipping information never seems to match the order. We don't know half the time what was shipped and what wasn't or when it happened. Besides, I've been trying to get authorization to extend the hours of the service center because many of our customers are on the East Coast and overseas. Our 7 A.M. to 6 P.M. hours in California aren't enough. We're trying to sell into Asia. By the time Singapore comes to work, we've gone home and vice versa. You can't solve everything with a FAX machine, you know. Also, we could use a couple of operators who are bilingual.

Accounting Manager: All we can do is process the data we're given. When sales and shipping take forever to get us data, what do you expect? Besides, that sales order form you've been using is really out of date. It has more margin notes on it than anything else. No wonder there are errors in billing and shipping.

Shipping Manager: Sure, blame the last horse over the fence. Everything that goes wrong is blamed on shipping. If you would get off your fat chairs and come down to the shipping dock some day, you'd see the problem. We ship over four hundred small items daily. Manufacturing leaves us out of stock, sales sends in incomplete or wrong orders on forms that are hard to read — then they are always making last minute changes and we have to break down the shipment and repack it. That ups the odds of errors being made. And if that wasn't enough, we have to work with a warehousing system that is chaotic. My people have to travel a city block and crisscross the warehouse to pick items. The shipping department was laid out by my predecessor twenty years ago when we had thirty, not four hundred, items to process. Is that enough or do you want more?

Procurement Manager: Well, don't blame it on us. We've been telling you for a year that the information flow is inefficient but you won't give us any help in making it better. I can't get budget to hire a consultant to rework my process. I talked to a couple of procurement managers last month at the national material conference. They told me about how they had gotten a group together to share data on better processes. They call it benchmarking and I'm going to try that; but don't expect miracles overnight.

Management Information Systems (MIS) Manager: Oh, yeah! Everything is an information problem these days, isn't it? We've got conflicting data coming in from a lot of sources on different time bases. So, naturally they don't match up. And I've been telling you that your homegrown PC programs don't always talk to each other. Now, you expect us to unravel it and make it work. It's like arranging a bowl of spaghetti in parallel lines. We've got to look at how other people are dealing with this problem. Are they centralizing or decentralizing? How do they use networks and standardize software? I need some fresh ideas and I'm not getting them here.

Human Resources Manager: The reason I can't fill position requisitions quickly is that corporate policy calls for eight approvals on any exempt-level req. What with travel schedules and other delays we spend the first five to six weeks just getting the req approved so we can start sourcing. Chief, I doubt that the world-class companies you're always talking about have the same policy.

Every problem discussed at Typically, Ltd. is ripe for benchmarking, a process by which a company compares its practices and procedures to those of the best companies to identify ways it can improve. The critical issue that must drive benchmarking is the opportunity to add value. Many benchmarking projects focus first on a process problem and take only a cursory, nonspecific look at the potential for value added. The key to optimal success in benchmarking is first to identify a major business opportunity or problem — for example, loss of market share — and backtrack through the outputs of the various functions to the processes that affect that value issue, then to benchmark the processes and trace the changes back through the outcomes to value added for the customer and thereby to the company.

My objective in this book is to link the driving business imperatives of vision and value to benchmarking. I will do this by providing a foundation for value management, by discussing the use of metrics in benchmarking to validate best practices, and by using a benchmark process model supplemented with examples from actual cases. To provide continuity and to illustrate the model, I will outline the phases of a hypothetical benchmark case (Sample Co.) in Chapters Four through Seven. In addition, Typically Ltd. will be referred to throughout the text to illustrate key learning points. The last two chapters will describe various types of benchmarking projects with which the Saratoga Institute has been involved.

The value model is distinguishable from other models of benchmarking in that it is intensely value driven rather than primarily process focused. Although some would disagree, I believe that benchmarking is ultimately about adding value rather than about process. We look at processes in our search for ways to add value, but our focus must shift from activity to goal. We engage in benchmarking because we seek to add value, not because we love the process of benchmarking per se. Organization development is an example of a methodology that has failed to live up to its potential because many of its practitioners love the process so much they refuse to define and measure the value obtained. It is my hope that benchmarkers will not fall into the titillating trap of activity for activity's sake. I want to help people avoid the mistake of benchmarking something that does not contribute optimum value. One of the greatest potential sources of increased value in a company is its staff processes.

Benchmarking Staff Processes

This book is directed specifically toward benchmarking staff departments. My working definition of staff includes just about every function except research and development (R&D), manufacturing, and sales. There is great hidden value within staff departments. When staff groups perform effectively they leverage the effort of their internal line customers toward outputs of greater value. When professionals fail to provide their product or service in a timely manner and in a high-quality configuration, the work of the line is adversely affected. The power of the staff to leverage value is virtually limitless. If we can find the best ways to account financially for the business; collect, configure and transmit data; support the human assets; maintain facilities; purchase material and equipment; and manage marketing, we will have made major contributions to our company's competitive position in the world market.

How Staff Functions Create Value

The traditional business model holds that if employees are not engaged in doing research, making the product, or selling it, they are what is called overhead, and overhead is expense, not value. Expense is to be tightly controlled and, whenever possible, minimized. In the best-run traditional companies, those functions or activities that do not add apparent value become targets for extreme cost control or even elimination. Almost all businesses are run under this mistaken, unexamined belief that staff are an expense. This outmoded tenet is based on ignorance, obstinacy, and complacency. In today's extremely competitive marketplace it is flat-out stupid.

Staff Leverage

Staff departments are the levers that line functions rely on to be able to operate at an optimum level. Figure 1.1 is a graphic example of the support leverage that staff departments apply to the company's operating units. If you have trouble seeing the relationship from a positive angle, look at it from the opposite perspective: Do you remember how people stopped working the day the air conditioning went out and the office temperature soared into the eighties? Do you recall how much time you wasted placating your staff when the new payroll system screwed up their checks? Will you ever forget how frustrated you were

Figure 1.1. Staff Performance Affects All Functions.

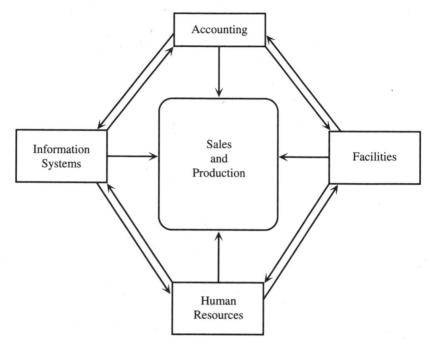

Source: Used with permission of the Saratoga Institute.

with the MIS programmers who overran your budget and schedule and then gave you a program that was full of bugs? Remember how angry you got when the recruiters took nearly four months to fill one of your key positions?

Those are examples of reverse leverage, cases where the staff hurt the organization. Someone in a staff department failed to perform his or her duties promptly or correctly and the customer, in this case you, lost productivity, faced morale problems, or blew the schedule and budget. Every manager has had to deal with these kinds of problems. The question is, if we can remember instances when a staff function was done poorly and we can pinpoint the negative effects, why do we have so much trouble seeing the positive, value-adding side of staff work? The answer must be that we are not looking for examples of how well-run staff departments add value.

The Value Path from Staff to Line to Customer

There is no question that staff add tangible value, directly or indirectly, to the bottom line. Everyone who sincerely looks for it finds it. The simplest example of this is the value path that can be traced from a staff department's work to the value added for the ultimate, external customer, as shown in Figure 1.2. When a staff department delivers its product faster, with fewer errors, and fulfills all the requirements of its internal line customer, it necessarily helps the line process. Instead of starting from behind with service that arrived late or had to be redone, the line function can carry out its value-adding process and deliver a better product, sooner and at a lower price than before. The best-run companies understand the flow and have identified the value added by the staff. If you cannot buy this argu-

Figure 1.2. Staff-Line-Customer Value Path.

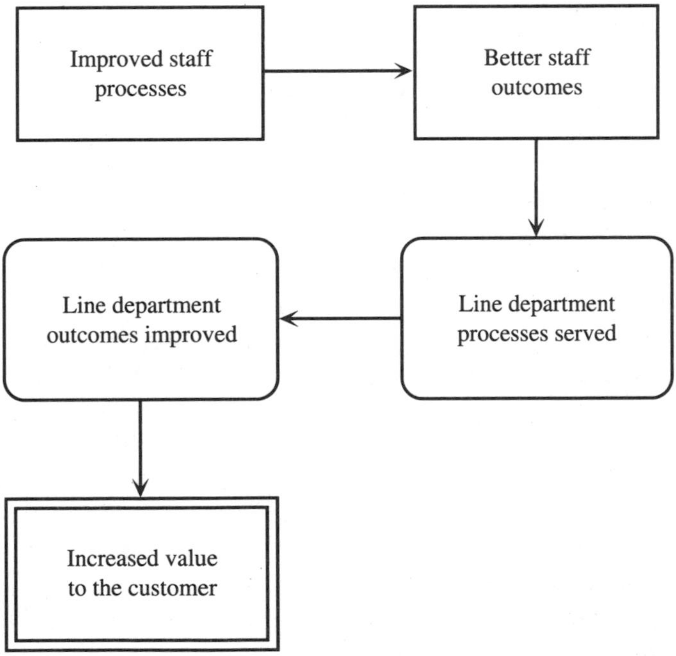

Source: Used with permission of the Saratoga Institute.

ment, review the other perspective: What is the loss when the staff department fails to deliver as planned?

To shift the traditional view of the staff department as an expense center, you have to change the way you think about the purpose of the staff. A new vision of staff is needed in today's market. Ask this basic question, Does management hire the staff in order to spend money? Probably not, because they already know how to do that in the line. They establish staff groups in order to add some type of value. If they want to identify that value, all they have to do is ask themselves why they set up the function in the first place. Was it to process paper or was it to achieve some type of tangible result such as expediting a shipment, facilitating the design of a new product, or speeding up sales? The result, when transformed into dollars or customer satisfaction, is the value. To find the value of staff department improvements, you have only to dig into the requirements of the line department customer. When you begin examining these interrelations, you will find that your new vision of staff is part of the larger company vision.

The Value Vision

It is currently fashionable for authors of management books to call for the development and communication of a vision. There has always been a need for a corporate vision. Employees look to top management to clarify for them what the organization is about. This is a natural desire. Employees want something of value around which they can rally. A vision will always be needed to focus the attention and energy of the human assets of an organization. It sets them off in a given direction; it motivates them to pursue excellence, to persevere during hard times; and it challenges them in good times to even greater performance. In effect, corporate visions define the playing field and provide a strategic-level scorecard. My vision is to add value to customers and employees. Without a clear understanding of value creation, all work, including benchmarking, is in danger of falling into the activity trap.

Every generation of North American managers since

World War II has been taught to manage activity rather than value. Strategic plans of production, sales, and administration business units are often focused on short-term gross volume improvements rather than on long-term value building. They reward on the basis of quantity rather than on value added. From the lowest positions to the executive suite, performance management systems have been skewed toward activity and short-term gain. This is one of the principal reasons more than half of the quality programs in the United States have failed to achieve their original goals.

Value for the Employee

All employees want and need a clear idea of the goal. Without a long-term objective they have no basis on which to make decisions. Yet, the simple, incontrovertible reality is that many employees have little idea of the value of their activity. They literally do not know what they should be doing or what is most important to do. They have no vision of their purpose beyond the processing of things or people and find their work unstimulating. All of us, from the least to the most talented, naturally want to be proud of our work. But we cannot find a source of pride within the endless production of something in which there is no perceived value. Assembly work, processing, and even professional outputs that don't add perceived value are joyless exercises for human beings. The lack of vision in companies has led to increases in employee stress, frustration, and alienation. It is very difficult, if not impossible, for employees to perform at consistently high levels when they do not see the value of their labors. And when employees are alienated, it is a dead certainty that the ultimate, external customers will be dissatisfied with their product or service.

Value is the heart of organizational purpose. Activity is the process by which value is created. We have only to look at the automobile industry to see how this truism went awry to the detriment of everyone from management and labor to the customer and, finally, the national economy. First, the U.S. automobile industry steadily lost market share from 1960 onward because management and labor fought for three decades over nonvalue-adding issues. Labor's original raison d'être was co-opted by management by the 1970s. If we ask what value the union has added to the worker's life in the past twenty years, we understand why membership has declined by over 50 percent. Concurrently, management failed the employees when they propped up executive stock-option values and declared dividends to stockholders while simultaneously refusing to reinvest in modern plants and management practices. Even though the signs had been around for twenty years, only in the late 1980s did both sides acknowledge that workers had given up trying to find meaning in their work.

Value to the Customer

If companies are to return to questions of value, to meaningful work and a corporate vision, they must get back to fundamental tenets. American management philosophy has always been based on the belief that the stockholders are the legal owners of the company. Without their investment of capital, the company would never have been founded or funded. My discussions with Japanese executives have confirmed stories in the popular press and recent management books that the Japanese believe that employees effectively are the owners of the company. Without their investment of energy and commitment the company would die. People, not capital, are the lifeblood of an organization. All this notwithstanding, I have come to believe that the customers are the true owners of the company. Only the customers can describe the value created by the investment of financial and human capital. Customers subjectively and objectively define the value requirements of the enterprise through their purchases. When customers turn away, they effectively sell their interest in the company. If enough of them turn away, the company is bankrupt. There will be no employees. The company will no longer have value as an enterprise.

A prime example of misplaced values comes from a service industry: airlines. The business executives and labor leaders in this field should have understood that they are not in the mass-production business. Shortsighted airline executives talk about customer service while they engage in repeated price wars that bathe income statements in red ink and produce no change in market share. Paradoxically, and despite advertisements to the contrary, they ignore the only differentiating weapon at their disposal: customer service. The case of TWA makes the point. Carl Icahn (formerly CEO and chief stockholder) tried to make the airline profitable through financial manipulation rather than through top-notch service. This position alienated the employees, who turned away customers, and in the space of five years TWA went from being a very good airline to bankruptcy.

How Customers Define Value

Value is a subjective term. Value is defined by the customer whether that person is outside the company or is an internal customer of a staff department. Each customer defines it somewhat differently. To claim that value is synonymous with customer satisfaction may be correct, but it is simplistic. Internal and external customer satisfaction results from the interaction of expectations and realizations, which are dynamic, idiosyncratic, psychological functions.

Customer expectations are often complex and partially hidden, even from customers themselves. Expectations are a combination of cost, time, quantity, quality, and human factors. The relative importance of these factors is continuously shifting. Sometimes the shifts are small and inconsequential. Other times they flip 180 degrees. What was valued yesterday will not necessarily be valued tomorrow. There is an endless list of companies, industries, political parties, and social institutions that have failed because they did not recognize this instability.

Most of the time value is a combination of factors. For some customers it may be a certain mix of convenience and cost that is defined by the location of the service, the time required to complete the transaction, and a fair exchange of money for product value. The fast-food business is based on those factors. People who frequent the drive-up window of the local hamburger palace are not expecting haute cuisine. They want a quick meal at a reasonable cost served according to a consistent formula. Consumers who want a pizza delivered are willing to pay more for the convenience of not having to go out and for the certainty of receiving their meal within thirty minutes.

If you want to build value, you have to know where it starts. Clearly, the customer does define the values desired. Knowing how to build value into your operations is the key to survival, competitive advantage, and success. Some people think it starts with good systems. Others press for motivation. Those are components but not the genesis of value. Benchmarking must focus on value added if it is to become a useful management tool.

The Wrong Question

The lesson for value seekers is deceptive in its simplicity. Most would say that finding value is only a matter of asking the customer what he or she wants and then delivering it if we can. The problem with this approach is that customers cannot always accurately define what they want in products or services. Marketers often struggle with this conundrum. They ask customers what they want in a product or service and they get an answer. The design and production units churn out the supposed solution and no one buys it. The mismatch is serious and perplexing, and is not confined to the public market.

Inside companies this same puzzle can appear when a staff department goes to its customers. The staff group displays its catalog of products and services and asks the line customers what they want. The line customers respond. Armed with this unchallenged data, the staff responds to the requests only to find the customers are still unhappy. Now the staff feels betrayed and unappreciated and the line workers believe, rightly so, that the staff does not understand the needs of the business. Why does this happen time and again? The problem stems from asking the wrong question.

Benchmarking projects frequently make this error. Someone assigns a topic to a benchmarking team. The topic may be broadly stated. The effects of solving the problem are not well thought-out, calculated, or documented. It is another "activity" to be pursued. The critical success factors, as the benchmark experts call them, have not been identified. As a result, when the project is completed the customer is unhappy with the results. Everyone just fell into the irrelevancy pit.

The Right Question

When considering a benchmarking project, we have to ask the right question. It is not, What do you want to benchmark? That is a focus on activity, not results. The right question is, What needs to be improved within your operation in order to obtain optimum value for your customers? If that turns out to be an identifiable work process, we then ask what the expected outcome of the process should be versus what it is now. We start by evaluating the result and then work backward to learn the location of the process deficiency. If we cannot just fix it, then we might consider a project to benchmark the process. But don't ask the staff manager what needs to be benchmarked. You can spend a great deal of time and money gathering information on how someone else proceeds, only to find that the manager was either (a) simply curious or (b) felt that he or she had to say something to get you out of the way so that the staff could go back to work.

There are at least two reasons customers often cannot tell suppliers what they truly need or want. One is that when some degree of technology is involved, laypeople usually cannot describe to the staff technician or professional which of their products or services will solve the problem or fullfill the need. We are simply unqualified by knowledge, education, or experience to make the judgment. When we go to the doctor with an illness, how many of us know which medicines we should ask for? When we go shopping for a car how many of us know which size engine is most appropriate for our own driving requirements? How many average citizens know what combination of disk drives and software packages we want when we visit a computer retailer? All we really know is what we want to achieve, not what it should take to accomplish our goal. Getting us what we need is the provider's job, right?

In the case of the doctor, we desire to be healthy again. From the car dealer we may want status, economy, or reliability from our vehicle. We visit the computer retailer because we need a word processing tool, not a lecture on Boolean algebra. Most of us only want to fulfill a specific need. We often do not know or care about the technology that makes that happen.

The other most common reason customers cannot tell suppliers what they need is that the customer is focused on his or her problem, not on the supplier's service. In fact, if we are honest with ourselves, customers really do not want our product or service, per se. They want their needs fulfilled and the two issues are not always synonymous. The supplier is a means to an end. The supplier's service is merely a tool or a path to help customers reach their goals.

When we apply this lesson inside the organization we come to realize how staff groups sometimes go wrong. For example, when someone needs to capture, maintain, or manipulate certain types of information they are not interested in the mystical workings of management information systems (MIS). They simply want to configure data in a certain format at a certain time to prepare reports or make decisions. When a line manager needs to hire, pay, or train an employee, the arcane technology of recruitment is not a subject of compelling interest. The manager simply needs a quality human being, who is paid competitively, is capable of learning and performing the responsibilities of the job, and can fit in with the work group.

The most useful question the supplier or a benchmark consultant can ask the customer is, What are you trying to achieve? Along with this are corollaries such as What other forces are at work on you? What are your problems and opportunities? Who is pressuring you? We have to diagnose the customers' health, so to speak. If we want to service their desire to be healthy, we have to learn what is making them sick. Does the problem or opportunity rest on cost, time, quantity, quality, or human factors? What combination of those factors can we prescribe or deliver to help the customers be healthier and happier? And finally, will benchmarking help?

It is always the responsibility of the professional to do the diagnosis. Whether the activity is sales, customer service, R&D, production, or any of the staff support functions, the question of desired value is answered through a dialogue led by the professional, not by the customer. This implies that the professional has certain skills, experience, and insight. He or she must learn enough about the customer's business to be able to ask the right questions and understand the answers. If there is a technology or a professional jargon, it must be mastered to some degree. If there are unique field conditions, they must be understood. Only then can the staff supplier ask the question that will yield a true and complete description of the factors that will create value for the customer.

In benchmarking, these characteristics of the business are called performance drivers. They define which companies are similar enough to become useful benchmark partners. During one benchmarking project in which the 3M Company was paired with a number of both larger and smaller companies, it became clear that the way 3M carried out research relationships with universities was organizationally impractical as well as financially impossible for the smaller firms. Therefore, the benchmark of 3M practices was of little use to the others.

For almost any function, however, it is possible to find companies that are suitable as benchmarking partners. With an effective process to observe, you can easily see the interconnection among the elements of the process and the value that it ultimately produces. This is the value-adding chain.

The Value-Adding Chain

Building value is a function of a five-link chain, as shown in Figure 1.3. This chain links the corporate vision and its human and material assets to the customer's requirements. Any weak link in the value chain breaks the bond between the business and the customer.

Culture is the first link. The chain starts with the acknowledgement of certain internal corporate, business unit, or department cultural values. This leads to the development of relationships within the organization between units affected by each

Figure 1.3. The Value-Adding Chain.

```
┌──────────────────────┐    ┌──────────────────────┐    ┌──────────────────────┐
│ Culture              │    │ Systems              │    │ Performance          │
│ norms, values,       │──▶ │ operating,           │──▶ │ employee behavior    │
│ rituals, and         │    │ administrative,      │    │                      │
│ relationships        │    │ control, and reward  │    │                      │
└──────────────────────┘    └──────────────────────┘    └──────────────────────┘

┌──────────────────────┐    ┌──────────────────────┐
│ Results              │    │ Value                │
│ quality,             │──▶ │ competitive          │
│ productivity, and    │    │ advantage and        │
│ service outcomes     │    │ customer             │
│                      │    │ satisfaction         │
└──────────────────────┘    └──────────────────────┘
```

other's work. The cultural factors spur the people to design systems that fit the culture. When a corporation's vision and culture are out of sync, a fatal flaw is exposed. When a new CEO brings in a radically different vision, the culture must adjust. One of the more dramatic examples of this was British Airways (BA). The company had grown complacent because of its market-share dominance through the mid 1980s. Service and efficiency were slipping. Competitors made inroads on BA's markets, and profits disappeared. Colin Marshall came in with a vision of urgency and customer focus. His vision drove a wrenching change in the culture. As a result, BA is once again on track, highly competitive, and a powerhouse in world air transport.

Systems form the second link. Systems, policies, and program and service process designs direct employee and management behavior in the desired direction. Systems include all formal processes from job design and work flow to policies and procedure manuals, information distribution, accounting methods and practices, pay and benefits programs, and other elements that make up the framework of the organization. Systems are inherently powerful. Like a river they flow along taking everything in their path in one direction. However, like some rivers, some systems are lazy, winding, uncertain, slow flowing, yet still powerful enough to move everything caught in the current, including swimmers, in a given direction. Other rivers are more direct, deeper, stronger. When these are flowing in the right direction they establish a force of tremendously effective power through the corporate landscape.

A typical example of the power of the system was evident in a computer company in Silicon Valley. Certain people were, with and without malice, included in and excluded from the flow of various operating data. If one was not in the flow, one was most definitely out of the game. It became very difficult to function effectively or to influence decisions if one was excluded from this information system. To stretch the analogy, those who were excluded were out of the flow and literally "high and dry." The power of the information system was blatantly obvious.

The integration of systems with the culture initiate, and indeed dictate, what are deemed to be appropriate, value-generating behaviors. These behaviors coalesce into organizational performance — the third link. Motorola is one of the best examples of an integrated culture and system. Chairman Bob Galvin announced in the early 1970s that the company was moving to a participative management culture. He then supported this redirection with training and recognition systems and opened up access to the information needed by employees to participate in improving productivity. This shift positioned Motorola managers and employees to take full advantage of the quality initiative a decade later. Had Galvin simply proclaimed a new participative culture but not reinforced it with the systems required, there is no question that the company would have floundered rather than prospered. Such floundering is exactly what is happening in many companies with TQM programs. A quality consultant told me that about 75 percent of his work is fruitless because the CEO and senior management make proclamations and then fail to follow through with the necessary support systems and changes.

The fourth link in the value chain is the operating results. It is here that we see improvements in quality, productivity, and service. Lower error rates and shortened cycle times signal that quality is improving. Product and service unit cost reductions along with greater output from the same or less input are signs of productivity gains. Higher levels of customer satisfaction are indices of service improvements, and this is where benchmark metrics are found. A number of industry surveys on the market yield this type of data. By looking into these reports of operating results we can identify best-practice companies that might serve as benchmark partners for staff functions. Granted, staff operating data are less frequently published than sales and production data; nevertheless, for those sincerely interested in improving staff department performance, data are available.

The final link, value added, is the result of improved performance. A subtle but important point is that a causal link does not always exist between improved performance and market value. For example, if your company's product is out of date, improving the quality of internal information flow probably won't add tangible value. The value of such action is akin to making a good buggy whip or even the slickest CP/M-based software program: few people use them anymore. The point should be obvious. Every link of the chain should be examined for its impact on customer value. At Typically Ltd., the issue, described at the beginning of the chapter, is movement between departments. Each function should be supporting its internal customer by providing timely and accurate service. However, the opposite was happening and the result was loss of sales and market share.

This point brings us to one of the cardinal principles of benchmark planning. When deciding to benchmark a staff process, the driving question must be, Is this the most value-adding process we could improve at this time? Widespread failure to examine this question has caused me to write this book. I don't see it being asked very often. In the chapter on value planning, Chapter Four, we will go into this in depth, but first, we need to examine the relationship between value and quality, a word much used in business circles today.

Value and Quality

The most overworked term in the current management lexicon is *quality*. It is used to describe just about any process or result. As such, it has become a cliché for the inarticulate. Quality is just one type of outcome from operations and administration. The other two are productivity and service. Collectively, quality, productivity, and service should constitute value. Quality can relate to the worth of a product or of a service. Lately, it is also being used broadly as a rather vague descriptor of organizations, as in "XYZ is a quality company."

To differentiate between value and quality, I would point out that value is the more fundamental term. Organizations do not survive and prosper because they provide quality. Their reason for being is that they provide value to the customer. The value may be expressed in terms of quality, cost, quantity, timeliness, or some human desire. A compulsive devotion to quality can lead not to world class profitability but to bankruptcy. There are many young companies that started out with a good product and attracted a loyal following. However, when they spent too much time trying to build the perfect second product, the market window closed and the companies folded. They became high-quality failures. Udo Schulz, former CEO of paint equipment manufacturer Wagner, once told me, "I keep telling the engineers that I want progress, not perfection." We need to redirect our inquiry from quality to value. The issue is how to add value. One answer is through benchmarking.

How Do We Add Value Through Benchmarking?

The aim of this book is to help benchmark-project personnel in staff departments learn how to find opportunities to add value within the organization. The value may come from improvements in quality, productivity, or service. The principles that I will cover are applicable to any provider-consumer relationship. When I talk about a customer, I will mean any value-adding, provider-consumer relationship. Some companies differentiate between internal and external customers. I have been told by friends at Motorola that to them a customer is someone who gives the company money in exchange for its products and services. In internal supplier-consumer situations such as typically exist between staff and line groups, the consumers are referred to as clients. This is a useful distinction for Motorola. However, in a book focusing on principles and methods for adding value to any business relationship, continually having to distinguish between the two would be ponderous and not particularly valuable. Therefore, the word *customer* will be used inclusively here, referring to any user.

Types of Value

If we are to add value for our customers, we must understand the nature of value. Within an organization, values can be divided into three general categories: production, human, and financial. It is natural for improvements in value in the production and/or human categories to flow through to financial values. One might fairly ask how something could be of value to a commercial organization if it did not culminate in a financial benefit. This issue usually surfaces when we talk about human values. The simple answer is that if we do something of value for the employees, eventually it should have a positive effect on the organization. On one of my trips to Japan I encountered this belief repeatedly. There it is an act of faith for Japanese management. In the United States, the practical problem is how to trace the effect to the bottom line.

Production Values. Quality, productivity, and service are production value categories. Quality deals with error rates and cycle times. Productivity focuses on costs and quantities. Service covers customer expectations and perceptions. These three are not as mutually exclusive as they might seem. At a practical level they interact with each other. All of them are dependent on human behavior. Therefore, an improvement in some human value should flow through to production value. That is the assumption behind the alleged connection between employee morale and productivity, although that causal relationship has never been proven.

Human Values. A number of organizational attributes are categorized as human values. These can be created by employee benefit programs that provide economic and often psychological security for employees. Training programs and career counseling support personal growth. Employee communications programs provide information that employees need in order to feel secure or that they can use to make career plans. Prompt and accurate pay systems ensure that they will be paid on schedule. At an informal level, coaching by a supervisor is valuable for employees because it helps them become more productive, work better with others, improve work quality and productivity, or provide better customer service.

Financial Values. The category of financial values includes all the returns on (ROs): returns on investment, returns on assets, returns on equity. It also covers organizational issues such as market share and profit (net income). Financial values are the grist for the mills of economists, stock analysts, and business reporters, few of whom have any conception of what it means to run a commercial enterprise.

Value Building Blocks

The production, human, and financial factors are the building blocks of value. The combinations they make for each situation and each customer determine the value in that case. Quality, productivity, and service improvements are paths we follow to add value. The customer's perception is the true value, which ultimately is expressible in dollars. The change in apparent value is usually measurable at two levels. The first measure is, of course, the customer's opinion. If you were to survey customer satisfaction at two different times, you would find either no change or a percentage of change in either a positive or negative direction. The second level of measurement is the actual percentage of change in one of the five indices, or links in the value chain, described above. If you apply the indices to the quality, productivity, or service you are trying to improve, you can calculate a percentage of absolute change. But the final question of value will always be, What does the customer say and what is that worth to you? Benchmarkers should keep this at the front of their thinking and planning.

Measuring value change becomes particularly intriguing when the results of the customer survey and the field measurement move in opposite directions. Consider this possibility: How could it be that we improve something, such as the time to respond to customers, while all other factors remain unchanged, yet customers are less satisfied now than before? The customers aren't playing tricks on us. The problem arises because the customers' priorities have changed. In this case, the key issue may no longer be time. It could be cost or defect rate. Value is not only subjective, it is transitory. Since it is dependent on human judgment, and since the environmental forces acting on a person are dynamic and ever changing, it is logical that value is subject to constant revision.

Now, we can see how organizations get in trouble internally and externally when they assume value is constant. This is known as losing touch with your customer. American business started doing it big time when Charles Wilson, former chairman of General Motors, boastfully uttered the management stupidism that what is good for General Motors is good for the United States. Fortunately, management is beginning to pay attention to the customers again. Internally, the problem is the same. Staff departments have to get in touch with *their* customers: the other functional heads and the employees of the organization. It is no longer sufficient merely to crank out services. Now, each staff group must be the most cost-effective source available. In many organizations, line managers are allowed to purchase their services from the best source, whether that is within the company or elsewhere. The practice is called *outsourcing* and it is becoming more and more common. Some companies have already moved their staff functions outside and made them freestanding businesses. In the summer of 1992, International Business Machines (IBM) transformed its human resource function into a free-standing consulting company called Workforce Solutions. If it can sell its services to the company and eventually the outside market, it will stay in business. A unit that loses its value, however, will not survive.

Loss of Value

Value can be lost in two ways. One involves time/distance and the other involves exchange points. In the first case, the farther away from its ultimate user an action takes place, the more likely it is to lose value. For example, a report prepared by central MIS may not reach a salesperson in time to help with a sale. Or a communication prepared by the employee communications unit at corporate headquarters may lose its meaning by the time it reaches a first-level employee in a plant. The problem is that the corporate staffer in headquarters may be out of touch with the assembler on the plant floor. The same applies for other functions as well. Moving anything takes time, and time is the enemy of value. Time and distance inexorably consume value.

The corollary to time/distance is connection or exchange. These factors tend to act together. The farther something has to move, the more likely it is to pass through a greater number of exchanges. In electrical systems, every time current crosses a connection it meets resistance and loses strength. In corporations, corporate staff sends something to group. Group transmits it to division. Division hands it off to the department, and finally someone in the department passes it on to a customer or employee. What is the chance that the information that started out is the same information that ends the journey? Just as distance consumes value, every time information passes between people it stands the chance of being delayed or reinterpreted. The distance/exchange dilemma is precisely the reason staff departments are being moved from corporate headquarters to field divisions. The shift solves both problems in one stroke.

Inaccurate or late data can have diastrous results. At Typically Ltd., every time data moved from one department to another it deteriorated. The end result was traceable all the way to loss of market share.

Conclusion

The purpose of this chapter was to make two points that are the foundations for organizational management, which includes staff benchmarking: (1) value is an imperative, and (2) value is customer defined. The speed of change is so great today that yesterday's innovation is today's commodity. We can no longer capture and maintain large market shares by focusing on a product. Today, success lies in creating value for our customer, and staff is a major value generator.

The United States of America is the home of the cowboy and the gunfighter. Our mode of organizational management follows that loose, free-spirit model. If we have a dispute with our market we look for someone to shoot it out with. We still want to find the bad guy in the black hat rather than ask the value questions. This illogic is imbued in our psyches. It is the architect of our management style. We refuse to acknowledge that the enemy is within. To quote a famous folklore hero, Pogo, "We have met the enemy and he is us."

Administrators of the Malcolm Baldrige National Quality Award, which originally operated on the action model, did not realize the shortsightedness of the award process for the first five years of its existence. In the beginning, the award criteria focused on activity. The committee awarded points to companies for having programs and systems that generated certain types of data. The redeeming feature of the award program was that it required candidate companies to establish quality-related systems, but it did not demand to see the proof of results in terms of value for the customer. While defect rates may have decreased and cycle times may have shortened, no one asked how much value the customer put on them. Were the Baldrige companies working hard or smart? Were they achieving better but irrelevant results? Subsequent events suggest that some were just working harder, because within a year of winning the award they fell on hard times. Their attention had been so concentrated on *quality as an activity* that they lost touch with their market and customers.

The lesson is that the game is not inside the organization. The organization is like the practice field and locker room of a sports team. The planning, conditioning, practice, and preparation take place there. The game doesn't start until the team comes out on the field and engages its opponent. In business it starts when the company enters the market and engages the competition and the potential customer. Throughout the contest the team cycles players in and out, connecting with its plans, coaches, equipment, and the opponent. In business the movement is back and forth, connecting with internal systems and employees, and with customer needs. Staff groups are like minibusinesses within a market, which is the corporation. They have to apply the same thinking and strategy.

Adding value is the responsibility of every employee. Value can best be obtained by focusing people on customer needs rather than on products and services. This is as true for internal as for external customers. You may feel that I have beaten the value issue to death. However, based on what I have seen and heard while consulting in twenty countries, I cannot impress too much on American managers that if they don't adopt the value perspective, they simply won't be competitive in the rapidly developing world market.

Staff benchmarking fits in the value picture because it can be an efficient and effective tool in the pursuit of adding value, provided the customer's needs are known. Value-added benchmarking demands constant revisiting of the value question. Benchmarking is a method for reviewing how someone manages a process. To make benchmarking a productive exercise we have to ask ourselves this question: If we did something the way the so-called best-practice company does, how would that add tangible, measurable quality, productivity, or service value for our customers? In the benchmarking model that follows, we will talk about each of the four steps in the process—value planning, data development, evaluation, and action—from a value-adding perspective rather than merely from a process viewpoint.

2

Basic Principles for Successful Benchmarking: Avoiding the Activity Trap

What is benchmarking and how does it differ from other forms of data gathering such as surveying or competitive analysis? How can we do it better? This chapter addresses the nature of benchmarking — its expectations, potential mistakes, and payoffs. It describes how current benchmarking models compare and how the process of value benchmarking for staff functions is distinctive.

$\mathbf{B}$enchmarking is an investigative process that seeks out high-performing business units, inside or outside the company, for the purpose of learning how they have achieved their exceptional results. It is not a difficult or mysterious process. It just requires hard work.

Toward a Definition of Benchmarking

Webster's Ninth New Collegiate Dictionary defines a benchmark as "a point of reference from which measurements may be made" or "something that serves as a standard." The most often quoted definition is attributed to the CEO of Xerox, David Kearns: benchmarking is the continuous process of measuring products, services, and practices against the toughest competitors or those companies recognized as industry leaders. Boeing, Digital Equipment Company, Motorola, and Xerox benchmark each other's processes on a regular basis and have agreed on the following definition of benchmarking: a systematic approach to identifying the benchmark, comparing yourself to the benchmark, and identifying practices that enable you to become the new best-in-class.

Spendolini (1992) conducted a study of fifty-seven companies that regularly benchmark. He found forty-nine definitions, which he tried to summarize into a universally acceptable version. Upon testing it, he found that everyone opted for a slightly different description. Deciding that he did not want to spend his career looking for the perfect definition, Spendolini developed a benchmarking menu containing nine categories, shown in Figure 2.1. Most of the categories have a list of similar terms. The menu can be read from 1 through 9 as follows: benchmarking is a (1) continuous (2) systematic (3) process for (4) evaluating (5) business practices and (6) organizations that are (7) recognized as examples of (8) best-in-class through (9) organizational comparison. If you prefer, you can substitute the words in each category and come up with essentially the same definition. For example, benchmarking is an (1) ongoing (2) analytical (3) process for (4) assessing (5) operations of (6) institutions (7) acknowledged as (8) world class in (9) making organizational improvements.

You can see from these examples that the scope of benchmarking almost defies a simple working definition. Nevertheless, I will venture the following as an attempt to cover the basic points: benchmarking is the ongoing search for best practices that can be adapted to lead an organization toward superior performance.

Hallmarks of Benchmarking

Essentially, benchmarking is an organized method for collecting data that can be used to improve internal administration, product manufacture, sales efficiency, or service delivery. The first book on benchmarking was written by Robert Camp (1989) based on his experience with the process during several years at Xerox. Camp considered benchmarking a proactive process

Figure 2.1. A Benchmarking Menu.

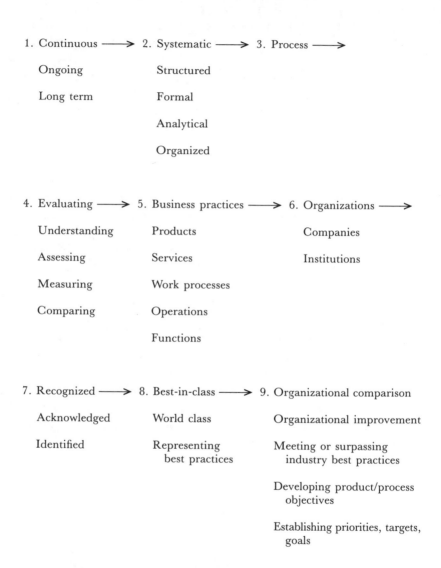

1. Continuous ———⟶ 2. Systematic ———⟶ 3. Process ———⟶

   Ongoing   Structured

   Long term   Formal

                          Analytical

                          Organized

4. Evaluating ———⟶ 5. Business practices ———⟶ 6. Organizations ———⟶

   Understanding   Products   Companies

   Assessing   Services   Institutions

   Measuring   Work processes

   Comparing   Operations

                          Functions

7. Recognized ———⟶ 8. Best-in-class ———⟶ 9. Organizational comparison

   Acknowledged   World class   Organizational improvement

   Identified   Representing   Meeting or surpassing
                            best practices   industry best practices

                                                   Developing product/process
                                                     objectives

                                                   Establishing priorities, targets,
                                                     goals

Source: Reprinted, with permission of the publisher, from *The Benchmarking Book* by Michael J. Spendolini, p. 10, © 1992 AMACOM, a division of the American Management Association. All rights reserved.

that can be used to help construct objectives based on observable, measurable facts. Others see it also as a tool that promotes learning and stimulates organizational change. Without benchmarks, managers tend to ascribe changes in customer requirements to history or "gut feeling" rather than to market realities or objective evaluations. This pattern applies as much to internal customer relations as it does to external.

Benchmarking is an externally focused, information-intensive process. It offers insights into better ways of responding to customer needs by collecting data from benchmarking partners regarding their approach to a given practice. The process is driven largely by objective, measurable data. It suggests stretching in the direction of the best known performance. Benchmarking is future oriented. It raises targets of excellence, stimulating people to match the best. This feature makes it action oriented.

Distinctions

Because benchmarking has just appeared on the horizon of many organizations' field of vision, it is often confused with other, more familiar forms of data gathering. Benchmarking is not the same as competitive analysis, surveying, or measurement. The differences are substantial although not immediately apparent to everyone.

Competitive analysis aims to ferret out hard-to-locate data regarding market conditions, trends, or competitors' plans or actions. One form of competitive analysis is business intelligence that describes what is happening in a region or around the world and the effects these events are likely to have on markets, competitors, or the company that commissioned the study. Competitive analysis is done out of the spotlight and may, on occasion, include clandestine data gathering. This secretive quality is one way in which competitive analysis is the antithesis of benchmarking, which is a cooperative process.

Surveying gathers data from a number of organizations. The surveyor usually computes and displays statistical means and distribution patterns of the data. In some cases the analysis identifies issues that need to be addressed because they show out-of-pattern scores. Surveying can be conducted within one company or across a large number of organizations—usually ones with similar backgrounds or interests. The most common types of surveys in business deal with compensation and benefits, opinions and attitudes, and general data such as technology applications. Surveys are almost always directed toward end results rather than toward processes or causes.

Measurement and benchmarking have come to be used interchangeably by some and this is causing a good deal of semantic confusion. The crux of the problem revolves around the use of the word *benchmark* as a noun rather than as a verb. As a noun, *benchmark* means a point of reference and may be either the measure of a result or the description of a process. An example is the often-quoted Texas light crude oil benchmark price of "$xx.xx" against which world petroleum prices are compared. When used as a verb, as in, "We benchmarked their accounts-payable practices," the term refers to the process of gathering and sharing data with other organizations about the way they all do something. The second term, *measurement,* may be used to show comparisons and to suggest relative values. Measurement is the recording and sometimes comparing of quantitative data. Measuring is usually a key part of a benchmarking project.

Benchmarking can take several forms. Data can be gathered primarily through telephone calls. They can be augmented with questionnaires and site visits to benchmarking partners. Gaps between the benchmark and each participating organization should be identified. Finally, metrics should be applied to the benchmark practice as a test to demonstrate that it represents a high level of performance. This last factor is often given short notice or is ignored in staff benchmarking. In such cases, any conclusions regarding the value of adapting the practice must be suspect.

Benchmarkers aim to locate organizations that do something exceptionally well. That something is the benchmark.

Then, to conduct a benchmarking project they develop a relationship with those organizations or business units, seeking to share data for the purpose of mutual learning. The focus is not on what happened. Rather, it is on examining practices and work processes, asking how and why the benchmark partners do what they do. Benchmarking aims to close the gap between one organization and the rest of the field. It assumes that having data on how the best do something will be useful in increasing the internal rate of improvement. Figure 2.2 is a graphic example of how benchmarking makes its point. The "Z" Chart shows the score plainly and objectively. It calibrates whatever gaps might exist currently between your organization and the best, how big the gaps are, and how they might change relative to one another in the future.

In applying this type of calibration, benchmarking can be much more useful than competitive analysis or surveying in providing directions regarding what needs to be improved and how fast. The three also might be used together. Competitive

Figure 2.2. "Z" Chart.

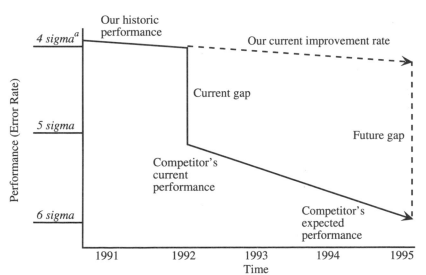

[a]A sigma is one standard deviation from the mean.

analysis might uncover some general intelligence on competitor movements or market trends. Surveys might sharpen the focus and gather additional information. Measures developed from a survey might pinpoint potential benchmarks as well as benchmark organizations. A benchmarking project might then be attempted to help close the gap between your company and the competition.

A Tool Rather Than a Solution

Benchmarking can be a very useful exercise to help a staff department add value within your company and for your customers, but it won't solve all organizational problems. If your company's market position is weak because of an operational flaw, such as poor customer service, benchmarking will generate data that may help you improve service. But if the problem is noncompetitive products, then benchmarking staff operations will not directly help you solve that.

Benchmarking can effectively accomplish the following:

1. Stimulate an objective review of processes, practices, and systems
2. Uncover and display the interconnections among different parts of the organization
3. Awaken the competitive drive of mediocre units
4. Provide outside objective data on methods of operation
5. Raise questions and identify potentially better ways of operating
6. Overcome the not-invented-here barrier to change
7. Support proposals for making change
8. Present a common target for improvement

Benchmarking does *not* (1) provide answers, (2) suggest priorities, or (3) prescribe action. A successful benchmarking project will leave you with a mass of potentially useful information regarding specific functions, processes, or practices. At its best, benchmarking will help you uncover root causes of problems or paths to exploit opportunities. Most operating-level problems, and for that matter opportunities, are of either a human or a system nature. If you have the right people with the right skills assigned to the right jobs, the problem is probably in the system. Benchmarking can provide the data you need to learn whether your internal systems, practices, or processes are flawed. It produces data, rather than opinions, that lead you in the right direction and point you to the solution. Then you must decide which external practices or processes can be adapted, not adopted, to add value within your unit.

Expectations of Benchmarking

To make benchmarking successful, you must understand what it involves. Calling up a few friends or professional associates and asking them how they do something is not benchmarking. Simply visiting those people and talking about how they do it may be useful, but it does not qualify as benchmarking. A true benchmarking project starts with the value question: What is the value in knowing something about this? The question leads to why you want to know it, what you would do if you knew it, and so on. The point is that benchmarking is not a casual activity.

Anyone who anticipates becoming involved in a benchmarking effort should know what to expect. One of the most common misconceptions I have encountered is that clients expect benchmarking to provide answers, and they expect the answers to be rather simple and easy to understand. This attitude is an example of the universal desire for the magic wand that will solve all problems. At the Saratoga Institute we have been helping companies develop quantitative benchmarks for fifteen years and we continually have to deal with the "should be" syndrome.

The "Should Be" Syndrome. The pattern of thinking that characterizes the "should be" syndrome appears in statements like these: "There should be a basic set of measures (preferably no more than five) that apply to all situations." "There should be one method that would work under almost all circumstances." "There should be a _____ (fill in the blank)." Given the makeup of this dynamic, complex world, there are not and there should not be such simple solutions. For simple solutions to exist for complex problems would be against the nature of such a universe. Everything is in balance: the more difficult the problem, the more complex the solution; the greater the potential gain, the greater the commitment of resources. Occasionally, someone appears to obtain through luck a reward far in excess of that person's contribution. Either we didn't see everything that went into it or the gain is only a manifestation of statistical probability. These cases are the rare exceptions. They represent one point at the end of the continuum, about umpteen standard deviations from the mean. For students of descriptive statistics let me explain that "umpteen" is one standard deviation beyond "zwelf."

Imitation. The search for the "should be" is a result of traveling the imitation path. Many people refuse to rid themselves of the "should be" syndrome. They believe that if they look hard enough they will find a result that they can imitate. This is the "find it and copy it" school of management and may arise from ignorance or indolence. In either event, it leads to disappointment or worse. When someone attempts to install another individual's or group's solution, he or she almost always fails. The very few times that this route produces a modicum of success, the cause is luck, not intelligence. The largest example of this management method occurred in the 1980s when many organizations became enamored with the Japanese method of quality management. People attended seminars and studied the literature that described and extolled the virtues of the Japanese methods. Ignoring the diametrically different cultural values and norms that made the system work in Japan, many managers tried to force fit the philosophy and methodology into American organizations. The results were predictable. The new system could not and did not work in the existing Western cultures. Benchmarking is not an exercise in imitation. It yields data, not solutions.

Learning. The most important point to grasp about benchmarking may be that it is a learning experience. Just as we go to school to learn how to do mathematics, we engage in benchmarking to learn how someone did something well. More important, if we are perceptive and insightful we might even learn why it worked for him or her. Mastering mathematics does not give us answers to specific problems. It gives us the method for solving problems. Likewise, benchmarking does not tell us what will work for us. Instead, it is a method for gathering data relative to solving certain types of value-adding organizational management problems. Peter Senge's book *The Fifth Dimension* (1990) describes successful organizations of the future as those that make continuous learning part of their system. Ongoing learning is the only way to keep up with a constantly changing marketplace. Staff benchmarking can play a central role in those types of organizations. It is a key tool of the learning organization.

Commitment. Benchmarking normally is not the so-called quick and dirty project. The commitment of time and resources is directly commensurate with the scope of the topics investigated. The Saratoga Institute has worked on small projects that looked at a few basic issues. It has also managed projects that explored a total function. In the first case a few phone calls, a simple set of questions, and basic analysis of data do the trick. However, in the latter type of project many people may labor several months and spend thousands of dollars to obtain the desired result. No one can tell you how much time it should take to complete a benchmarking project. That question is similar to asking how much time you will need to take a trip. Only after you know the distance, terrain, means of transportation, and so on can you give a useful and valid answer.

Beyond the commitment of resources there is a requirement to commit oneself. Skills must be developed, and the most important skill set is communication. Benchmarkers need to know how to ask questions, how to listen, how to grasp connections among the data being described to them. They also should know how to manage a project; how team roles are established, assigned, and played; how to acquire and manage support resources. Most important, benchmarkers must know how to obtain pertinent data and then be able to analyze them. Objective data management skills are not common. We have seen people from vice presidents on down sitting on literally piles of data and having no idea what they all meant. If you don't have analytic skills you need to find someone who has them, either within the organization or from an outside source. It is wasteful and counterproductive, not to mention extremely frustrating for everyone, to obtain a mass of data and not know how to interpret it.

Connections. The data from one operation reveal more than just what is happening within that unit. They also tell something about other operations. In a case like Typically Ltd., benchmarking one function is going to require relating the data produced in that project to the other functions as well. Clearly, every function in that case is connected to and has impact on several other groups. Each function is a stakeholder in several others. As data are obtained they must be reviewed, not only as they relate to the internal workings of the subject function — for example, shipping — but also as they affect other groups — such as MIS, customer service, and accounting.

One inherent strategic advantage that Asian companies have over Western companies is their holistic view of life. Western logic claims a thing is either A or not A. The Eastern perspective understands that everything is part of everything else. The world is one. Everything is related to A and vice versa. Benchmarkers will do well to keep the universal web of existence in mind as they try to understand their data.

Integration. The definition of benchmarking begins by making the point that it is an ongoing process. Most people view benchmarking as an occasional project in addition to their job. The full potential of benchmarking appears when it becomes part of doing one's job. It is only by continually benchmarking the best and implementing the knowledge gained that benchmarking's true value will be realized.

The value chain in Chapter One showed that for something to add value it must become part of the system, which is another way of saying that the learning must not only be applied, it must become part of the way of doing business. If left outside the work system and treated as a periodic occurrence, benchmarking will yield sub-optimal results. It needs to be part of the way we work. In the beginning, most organizations are not ready to make this incorporation. They first need to get a couple of small projects under their belt, so to speak. By learning the do's and don'ts of the process, they will acquire the skills and understanding that will make it easier to integrate benchmarking into the operating system. They will also gain self-confidence in knowing that they can add value through benchmarking.

Few things in life are as painful or constructive as experience. Trial and error is the way all beings learn. Eventually, when enough collective experience has been gained through individual projects, benchmarking can be rolled out to the total organization and integrated into the management system. Incorporation at this level will require training as well as support from top management. Support is defined here as rewarding people for using benchmarking to achieve better results. If management does not model the new benchmark and does not reward its use, benchmarking will not become an integral part of the system.

Metrics. Although benchmarking focuses on processes, there is a role for metrics as well. Performance measures or metrics are the scorecard. They tell you how well the benchmark partner has done and later, how well you are doing. They are used continuously in many functions such as sales and production. It would be absurd to suggest that we don't need to know how much the product cost to manufacture or what the dollar level of sales was for a given period. Nevertheless, many staff departments run with only the grossest and simplest of objective data.

This lack of data explains why staff groups are generally referred to as expense centers. They seldom show quantitatively what value they have added. Metrics are indispensable in benchmarking to overcome this shortcoming. First, you need them in order to know how your process is currently running. You also want to know how current figures compare to what you did in previous periods. Finally, if your benchmark partners don't have hard performance measures, you cannot tell if theirs is a best practice. One large benchmarking project produced unsatisfactory results because the process data could not be connected to any quantitative results. Some consultants downplay the value of metrics, but I don't see how you can benchmark without quantitative indices of process inputs and outputs.

Common Mistakes in Benchmarking

We all seem to make a number of mistakes when we start our first benchmarking project. I will talk about these problems throughout the chapters that follow, as I discuss the parts of the process in which they might occur. Nevertheless, it is useful to be able to visualize them all at once. If you are going to teach benchmarking to others, the following list can serve as a guide to common benchmarking mistakes to avoid.

- *Too broad in scope.* Everyone seems to want to take on the world.
- *Too many questions.* Start with a small list. It will grow as the project unfolds.
- *Team is not prepared.* Benchmarking may not be rocket science, but it does require some skills and preparation, and people do have to be committed to the project.
- *Haste makes waste.* Some mistake speed for quality. It is better to take time and do it right.
- *Metrics versus practice.* You need the numbers, but focus on the practices.
- *Partners are too similar.* The farther afield you look, the more likely you are to learn.
- *Famous-company fixation.* They may be good in some things but seldom are world-class in everything.

Why Benchmark?

Given the increasing demands brought on by heightened competition, requirements to control costs, and organizational and work changes, you might well ask yourself, Why should I get into this? — certainly a valid question. You want to allocate resources only to those efforts in which there is an identifiable value. Benchmarking potentially can produce substantial value in both expense reduction and revenue generation.

You might argue that you are already making improvements through your quality programs. The question is, are they coming fast enough? At Alcoa, incoming CEO Paul O'Neill reviewed the company's position and realized that quality programs alone would not generate the rate of change that was necessary for Alcoa to improve its share of the world's aluminum market. To supplement and energize the quality effort, in September 1991 he imposed a goal of closing the gap between Alcoa and Kobe, the world-class aluminum producer, on three basic indices by 80 percent within two years! His objective was to stimulate the competitive juices of the Alcoa people. He got everyone's attention. As of December 1992, Alcoa was moving rapidly toward achieving that goal.

Quality, productivity, and customer service programs can work well on small, easy-to-fix problems, but in a total quality management (TQM) program a full-scale organizational commitment is required to solve the larger value-adding problems. It normally takes at least one year and usually about three before top management begins to see the effects of a TQM effort on the bottom line. This lag explains why so few quality initiatives fulfill the expectations of management. Top management in the United States is notoriously impatient and fickle. In TQM, large supportive structures have to be built. Naturally, it takes time for those structures to begin to pay back the investment. Conversely, in benchmarking all attention can be devoted directly to a singular opportunity to add value.

Benchmarking provides the outside reference points, the benchmarks, against which the company is competing. It deals

not only with the *what* and the *how,* but also with the more important *why.* Benchmarking can be an important component of a
TQM program. It can bring focus to quality efforts. It can be an
important tool to drive quality in the most useful direction. Benchmarking should, but doesn't always, focus on the most important,
highest-value-adding issues. This deficiency is also a failing of
many quality programs. Quite often they become program ob-
sessed and expend large amounts of resources on inconsequential
issues. This misdirection can be avoided in benchmarking if the
issue of value is the driving criterion. Beginning with the first
planning step, benchmark only those opportunities that will
generate a significant, visible payoff. You get a lot more attention and support with one home run than with four singles.
Benchmarking is most useful when it investigates large-scale issues such as those discussed in the following paragraphs.

Strategic Level

Benchmarking can add value to processes such as strategic planning when it gathers data on how effective planners run their
process and what they look at. Our experience is that many people haul out the old planning models and go through the exercise with only the slightest vision of adding value. On the other
hand, there are some who clearly plan more effectively, as seen
by the value criteria and the methods they employ. A few of
the other macro issues that can be benchmarked include downsizing and restructuring processes, market positioning, and community or government relations.

Operations and Administration

Most benchmarking projects work at the level of operations and
administration. Project staffers look at the work-flow processes of
a function such as accounting in companies that are extremely
cost-efficient administrators. Staffers study relationships between an information services (IS) unit and its customers to learn
how the best-in-class optimize those connections. Studies of processes within facilities management, human resources, customer

service, marketing administration, security, public relations, controller, and treasury or other functions are typical projects. So long as they address significant opportunities these projects can add value. Typically Ltd. is an example of a company with operational and administrative benchmarking potential.

Special Purpose

Benchmarking can be applied to any issue for which there are available data, willing partners, and significant potential value. A short list of possibilities includes stimulating creativity and innovation, empowering first-level employees, restructuring, achieving crossfunctional cooperation, managing a diverse workforce, implementing performance measurement systems for professionals and managers, designing organizational communications systems, and managing environmental hazards.

How Benchmarking Pays Off

Benchmarking has many potential benefits. Some of these, such as the data generated, are expected, but others — like the benefits of teamwork — are bonuses.

Teamwork

One of the most enduring but least-noticed values of benchmarking is the effect a successful project has on staff relationships. After the project is completed, staff members reap the benefits of working on a winning team. Since the project team must work closely together for several weeks or months, they usually develop a team spirit as well as teamwork methods that they carry over into everyday interactions. As more people across the organization engage in benchmarking, the team skills and spirit gradually pervade the whole department.

Data

The most visible benefits of a successful benchmarking project are the data that it yields and the results of implementing the

data: the improvements. If the team has done its job well—
that is, has selected a high-value topic and generated penetrating questions—the end product should be information that can
be used to make substantial process improvements. Former
Xerox chief executive David Kearns has repeatedly claimed that
benchmarking literally saved the company when it was rapidly
losing market share in the early 1980s.

Evidence

Benchmarking forces people on the inside to look outside. It
combats the not-invented-here syndrome, and this is a major
benefit. In 1980, a television special entitled "If Japan Can Why
Can't We?" forced America to acknowledge that someone outside was doing better than we were. Furthermore, the message
was that if we didn't look, learn, and change, we would become
a second-rate economic power. Subsequent loss of domestic and
world market shares proved the point.

Partners

Another benefit is the relationships that develop from the contacts with the benchmarking partners. These contacts pay off
by assembling a group of people who can be called on again
as you all learn together. Benchmarking is a process of sharing and learning. You give, you take, and everyone wins. In
the summer of 1992, the Saratoga Institute helped to form a
group of training managers from twenty-six U.S. and Cana-
dian companies for the purpose of sharing data on how they
were measuring training effectiveness. This began as a project
and looks like it will become a permanent group. There is a
common interest in developing and applying a model for measuring the value of training and education outcomes. Such
groups existed within many industries and professional groups
long before benchmarking became the hot topic. Benchmarking now gives them a formal process for increasing the value
of their relationship.

Locating Benchmark Partners

The most difficult part of benchmarking at this point is locating useful benchmarking partners. Beyond a small number of well-known, high-performing companies, useful benchmarking partners are invisible. Diligent research is required to find them. Within a few years a number of sources will be directly dedicated to maintaining benchmarking data. These will be described in Chapter Four. Today, the search must take place across the general field of public information.

Before you go looking for benchmark partners you need to address two issues:

1. What is the purpose and objective of the benchmarking project? Why are you considering doing this? As the old saying goes, "If you don't know where you're going, any road will take you there."

2. What types of companies will make useful benchmark partners? This question brings up the issue of performance drivers, which will be covered in Chapter Four. Basically, you need to find companies whose performance drivers are most like yours. You can't compare processes between AT&T and West Overshoe Telephone Cooperative.

The good news on finding partners is that astounding amounts of data are available today on practically any subject imaginable. At last count there were more than ten thousand electronic bases in operation. There are so many data bases that there is even a data base of data bases. The question is not whether you can get the data, it's how you can do it as efficiently as possible. The only caution with data bases is that their information may be out-of-date. Also, you may not be able to learn how valid and reliable the data are. Just because something is in a data base does not necessarily mean it is true.

The United States is the greatest data bank in the world. We have a multitude of institutions that regularly collect and share data. The most prominent ones are found within the general and trade media and the financial services industry. Anyone who reads general business and economic news cannot help coming across data on organizations that are doing something well. A short list of information sources that might lead you to benchmarking partners would include the following:

- Government agencies, both U.S. and foreign
- General press, publicity, feature stories
- Trade press, magazines, newsletters, association newspapers
- Annual government-required corporate reports, such as 10-Ks and 10-Qs
- Special press, special interest magazines, newspapers, newsletters
- Company publications, product brochures
- Professional society publications, journals, newspapers, newsletters
- Financial institutions such as securities analysts and banks, particularly their economic departments

Beyond these formal sources you can also get leads by talking to people. Consultants, customers, suppliers, academics, and business friends all have contacts. They read and talk to other people. They can expand your scanning effort.

Source Locations

Essentially, a would-be benchmarker can turn in four directions to find benchmark partners and data: business units within your organization, external groups within your industry with which you compete directly, groups within your industry with which you do not compete, and other organizations that may be in different markets but have something of value to share. The advantages and disadvantages of the four are outlined in Table 2.1.

Internal

Internal benchmarking is not optional. It is the key point from which to launch a benchmarking project. Before you can start an external benchmarking project you have to know your internal system. The best way to know it is to compare it to other

Table 2.1. Benchmark Partner Characteristics.

Location	Advantages	Disadvantages
Internal	People usually known and a sense of common company goals shared Data easy to access Solutions easy to adopt since they fit your culture	Internally biased; not-invented-here Some cases not an identical function, for example, accounting versus benefits processing
Competitive	Comparable practices Background market conditions well known Data directly applicable	Data more difficult to acquire Ethical considerations Limited sharing
Industry	Comparable practices Data generally applicable Data easily shared	Background market conditions often not well known Size or geographic differences
Generic	Widest possible field for finding value No problems with data sharing Development of personal network	Difficulty in integrating findings Time-consuming Some data nontransferable

internal systems. This first step provides a spin-off value as the internal benchmarking partners gain knowledge that might help them to improve their processes. The disadvantage of focusing solely on internal units is that you are less likely to find a world-class example. Also, exclusive internal focus leads to the not-invented-here attitude that stifles innovation.

Internal benchmarking can yield several useful outcomes. It gives you the initial information needed to begin to truly understand your own process. Organizational problems that might have remained hidden are now exposed for someone to fix. It might identify an endemic problem from which several similar functions suffer. And later, you will do a better job outside because of your inside experience.

The internal benchmarking process asks the following questions:

1. What are we doing? Describe the key steps.
2. Why are we doing it? For what purpose?
3. Who is doing it (number and type of people)?
4. Why are *those people* involved? What value do they add?

Large organizations often have units scattered across divisions carrying out similar or identical operations. For example, high-volume processing can be found within accounts payable and receivable, payroll, employee benefit claims, information services, marketing administration, and purchasing departments, among others. In some cases, the data points and processes are nearly identical, which makes for good benchmarking. In other cases, a paper-flow process might be checked across functions. Since paper processing is a generic function, comparing accounts payable processes with benefit claims payments can be useful. This comparison would require some interpretive work to account for differences across the functions.

The biggest problem you are likely to have is with the management of the departments you want to benchmark. While some will see it as an honor that you have come to them to "see how it is done," others will feel threatened. When you approach your potential internal benchmarking partners, keep in mind that they might not be as enthusiastic about this as you are.

The experience of internal benchmarking will prepare you for an external project. You will know better what you need to know. You will have developed a list of key issues and questions that follow them. You will know what types of measures should be obtained to identify the effects of the process. If you keep your senses highly tuned you will pick up some of the constraints and the key performance drivers as well. These will be very important later when you are trying to determine which companies might be useful matches with which to benchmark.

Competitive

When benchmarking deals with internal staff functions, it is usually easy to benchmark with competitors. Accounting, facilities, information systems, human resources, and safety/security professionals often do not feel that they are directly competing in many areas with their peers in competitor companies. If the topic turns to customer service or marketing administration processes, however, the attitude can easily become defensive.

If you are able to obtain data from competitors, even if the information does not appear to be competitive, it does help you understand your competitive position. You may also find that your competitors want to join forces and learn together how to improve. An example might be that a group of small competitors would band together and benchmark large or medium-size companies. Or they would decide to benchmark foreign competitors who are entering their market. In one project, we discovered that a group of retailers wanted to benchmark certain employee-based costs. The big retailers did not want to share data with the small retailers and vice versa, but they were willing to share data with companies of their own size.

Competing companies can work together to strengthen their individual positions if the proper win-win attitude is established in the beginning. The key checkpoint in competitive benchmarking is making sure that you understand how your partners are structured. Structure is a critical performance factor. If, for example, they outsource payroll while you handle it internally and you are trying to get a handle on accounting costs, you might be very confused when the data come in. If you are looking at corporate administration, how centralized are they? Do they have a big law department or do they have most of their work done by outside counsel? Are the management information system/electronic data processing (MIS/EDP) functions all done in house or is some part of it outsourced, such as maintenance programming? Function by function, you need to know how they map out or your data may be misleading.

Noncompetitive

Often many of the companies within your industry are not competing with you. Examples of these are banks, hospitals, hotels, and other public service businesses that operate in different geographic markets. You may also find differences within product categories. If you produce electric motors of less than one horsepower, you are not competing with turbine manufacturers. You may make engines for lawn mowers, but not motor scooters. There is no reason for noncompetitive companies not to benchmark each other. No one can lose a competitive advantage.

On the positive side, noncompetitive companies may have common practices and problems. Data transfer rather easily. On the negative side, markets and customers may be entirely different. Burt and Ernie's Bank, a one-branch operation in West Overshoe, does not have much in common with Bank of America or Citibank. Another potential negative is that industries have their traditions. They have done certain things in certain ways for decades and have never questioned them. In fact, they often defend inefficient, even inane practices on the basis of tradition. So, it is less likely that you will find a world-class operation if you limit yourself to one industry. With noncompetitive industry benchmarking you are mostly interested in industry trends— macro issues that are affecting many companies within your industry.

Generic

In this context, the term *generic* means any other company. This is the arena of greatest opportunity. First, it is the largest group, because it can include anyone beyond the internal group. Second, it is the group among which you are most likely to find the best practices, in the world-class organizations. By looking outside your company or your industry, you have the greatest chance of discovering the freshest ideas. But beware of hype. At one time, a highly publicized computer manufacturer, a company with an excellent reputation for technology, couldn't cut a check in fewer than sixty days. Great effort had gone into technology and people management, while the accounting function . . . didn't.

A commonly applied method of generic, best-in-class benchmarking is for a group of companies with a common background to get together to look outside their industry for best practices that might be applicable inside the industry. Consider the case of a number of California biotech companies that were still relatively young and needed chemists, immunologists, and biologists. Most had not yet developed efficient methods for recruiting large numbers of highly degreed professionals. They approached a group of West Coast recruiters who had been recruiting physicists and engineers for electronic companies for nearly two decades. All of these companies were looking for highly skilled personnel but they were not looking for the same skills; therefore, they were not competing with each other. They traded information about college recruiting to learn how to work more effectively with college placement offices and faculty. The biotech recruiters learned volume processing methods, and the electronic recruiters heard some fresh ideas on working with student technical clubs and faculty.

The farther you go from your company and your industry, the more you have to pay attention to comparability. Do you match up well? Are your structures similar? Are your drivers similar? If they are not, which is more than likely, can you factor in the differences so that when the data come out you will truly understand them? Take care that you don't benchmark a company just because it has a good overall reputation. If you are a relatively small company, it may be titillating for you to visit the halls of a megacorporation, but it may also not be worthwhile.

What does it take to be best-in-class or world class? Good question. Chapter Nine tells the story of a best-practices project and what we discovered. Does *best* mean that the company has no problems? Does it mean that it can stop trying to improve? Of course not. It simply means that a company currently has a competitive advantage over about 90 percent of other companies in the field in one given function.

A prime barrier to effective benchmarking is the need that some people have to defend their methods. Make it clear in the beginning that you are not assuming that anyone is ineffective. The purpose of the project is to learn how we can all be better so that we can compete, survive, and be highly successful. All of us have room for improvement in our operation. It is in everyone's interest to be the best we can be.

Differing Approaches to Benchmarking

It is not my intention to tell you that I have *the answer* to all benchmarking projects or to suggest that my views are better than those of others who have managed a number of projects. Although benchmarking is still in its early stages of development, there are already several established models: IBM, Xerox, DEC, Federal Express, AT&T, Florida Power and Light, and others have their benchmark models. While they all cover basically the same steps, each model is somewhat different from the others in form but not in intent. Some are more detailed than others. One emphasizes certain aspects and another emphasizes others. Camp's Xerox model (1989) laid out ten steps in four phases. IBM and DEC both have fourteen steps in five and four phases, respectively. Spendolini's hybrid model (1992) requires a large amount of time for formal reporting. Leibfried and McNair (1992) hardly touch on it. From a user standpoint, it doesn't matter which model is applied as long as everyone on the project understands the one selected.

The Value Benchmarking Model

The benchmarking method used by the Saratoga Institute aims to achieve the same general results as the other methods, but it differs significantly from them in two very important ways: the value orientation and the link between the staff and the customer. As such, this approach makes certain that whatever we benchmark, we are going to add value for the customer and thereby gain competitive advantage.

In the beginning of benchmarking, most models were linear. Now a circular model is considered most appropriate, given the desire to make benchmarking a continual practice. The linear models include a feedback loop at the end of the process, but the motion is not continuous. Once a project is completed, the change has to be institutionalized before another project can start. Only when benchmarking becomes part of the management system will it be a continuous process. Figure 2.3 is an illustration of this value process model.

Figure 2.3. The Value Process Model.

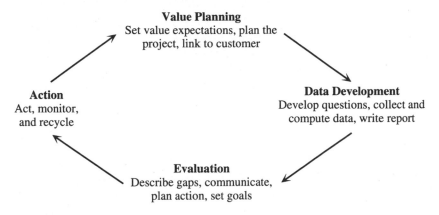

In practice, the process oscillates back and forth across the four steps. It is somewhat akin to alternating current, where the energy flows in one direction and then reverses itself and flows back toward the source. This constant recycling makes benchmarkers continually check to ensure that they are still servicing the values defined at the first step.

The first step in the institute's model is significantly different from other models. Our initial step is anchored in a search for value. Where nearly all benchmark models start with identifying what is to be benchmarked, we start at a more fundamental level, with value planning. In most models, critical success factors are prescribed as key steps. However, practice will attest to the fact that these factors are often neglected, stated much too broadly, or not accurately assessed. In such cases, the focus drifts through activities, causes of problems, or internally prescribed measures of performance that may have become irrelevant in the fast-changing market. This lack of value identification echoes the typical American approach known as Ready, Fire, Aim.

I believe that part of the American problem of poor analysis is that, as cowboys and cowgirls, we admire action more than thought. Outside of finance and engineering, our educational system doesn't teach good analytic skills. Some staff people understand accounting and statistics but they don't grasp the interactive nature of quantitative organizational operating data. I once attended a meeting of software professionals who agreed they were great at mathematics but useless when it came to understanding organizational dynamics data.

In our approach, value planning is the first, unavoidable prerequisite. The prime question is, What value are we going to get out of this? The corollary is, Is that the greatest value we can obtain right now? Nothing happens until the different values have been identified and ranked. We dig deep to find where the potential value is as well as how it compares to other potential values. Our experience at the Saratoga Institute is that many management actions, including benchmarking, are launched without a clear notion of the potential value of the expected outcomes. Because of this fuzziness, the result is often an expenditure of resources with little identifiable value at the end. If we do not have a target that is somewhat quantifiable in terms of expected values, how will we know if we are making the best use of our time? This missing value step causes much of the fruitless activity that pervades organizations.

The second distinction is that we always try to link the learning to serving an ultimate need — value obtained — for the client's customer. Rather than focus on and stop at the practice or process being benchmarked, we urge clients to carry it one step further and define the linkage between the expected outcome and the value for their customers. We claim that benchmarking is not about process, it is about adding value. We don't want process for the sake of process.

We believe that although the strong value imperative and the oscillating style of continual rechecking for value make the value benchmarking process seem somewhat difficult, it is actually easier and certainly more fruitful than some of the earlier models. The difference is not so much in the steps as in the reasoning behind the steps: the why and how. As my wife constantly reminds me, "Jac, it isn't so much what you do that matters as how you do it." The constant value question that is embedded in the process makes it easy for benchmarkers to stay on track and yields a better end result.

Conclusion

In this chapter I prepared the foundation for benchmarking by addressing the key issues surrounding it. The objective was to move the reader from the value imperative toward the process of benchmarking.

The best advice anyone can give you regarding benchmarking is to keep it simple. We tend to overcomplicate our lives and our work, which only increases the odds against being successful. I'm certain that somewhere in the book of natural law there is an algorithm that says something like this: "Every time we add one more variable to the process, the risk of failure rises by a factor of ten."

Be realistic. Benchmarking is not a magic wand. It will not give you the one best way to do something. All you can expect is that it will raise good questions. Someone once told me that the answer to any problem is found within the question. Learn to ask the right question and the answer becomes obvious.

Start focused. People want to get too much out of a benchmarking project. Often they try to cover too much ground and ask too many questions. Too much data can be as big a problem as too little data. After they have collected a mountain of data, people seldom know how to sift through it to find the kernels of value.

Prepare carefully. Your success is directly dependent on the team's skills, experience, and level of interest and on your partner's ability and willingness to share useful data. To the extent that people on either side are not ready, the project will fail to reach its highest possible success. Team members must not only buy into the project, they should also help sell the results to the organization. Partners must be good matches or the data will be useless. Spend time and your best efforts in preparation. To paraphrase the old saying, "An ounce of planning generates a pound of results."

Think long term. Use of benchmarking is increasing. It is a very appealing process. People usually like to talk about how things work, and they especially like to talk about how their own methods are working well. There are many benefits to be obtained from benchmarking, including, naturally, the data and other obvious benefits. But probably more important in the long run are the interpersonal and management skills that participants acquire through benchmarking projects. I think the best result is that the relationships that develop will pay off in many ways for a long time. Finally, if you keep benchmarking focused on adding value for your customers, you will gain a great deal from your efforts.

3

Performance Measurement: Applying Numbers in Benchmarking

Benchmarkers need quantitative data with which to distinguish best practices from others as well as to measure the results of their efforts. Unfortunately, many business people in the United States are not strong in quantitative analysis. By taking a value-adding perspective and tracing the route from staff processes to customer value, they can generate the data needed and easily understand what it implies.

Benchmarking focuses on processes but numbers or metrics are needed if the outcomes of the processes are to be evaluated. Without quantitative measures of outcomes it is very difficult to draw conclusions regarding which process yields the best results. In this chapter, I will display and describe the measurement system the Saratoga Institute has been using with clients over the past fifteen years and show how it fits into benchmarking.

Measurement in Benchmarking

A fundamental truism of business is that you get what you measure and reward. It has a corollary: the only thing that cannot be measured in business is a concept. Concepts are invisible, but every person, piece of work, or human reaction is susceptible to being measured. The only question is, what is worth measuring? Examples of concepts are leadership and management. We can't see leadership. What we see is a series of actions and the responses of the employees; collectively, we call this leadership. We can measure the actions and responses in terms of some combination of cost, time, quantity, quality, or human reaction. The key to performance measurement is to make the target visible. Measures can conceal as well as reveal. Care must be taken to pick the right thing to measure.

A secondary point regarding performance measurement is that people not only like to know how they are performing; they also have a right to know. In a study carried out several years ago, we asked nearly four thousand employees at all levels of a dozen companies what they most wanted to have communicated to them by their company. The two most wanted items, which were statistically above all others, were evaluations of job performance and information on career opportunities. Performance measures are needed to guide and evaluate individual and group performance. Without them, we generate ambiguity and anxiety, neither of which are conducive to improvement.

In this section, we will look at the three levels of organizational phenomena — processes, outcomes, and impact — and link them to the value added by positive changes in impacts. While we will study each level separately to simplify understanding, in practice there is obviously some overlap and interaction of performance indices. For example, when you improve quality indicators you will probably have an impact on productivity and service indices as well. The workplace is composed of interactions and interdependencies. This discussion will provide several ways to isolate and measure them, individually and collectively.

Several well-known management consultants such as Peter Drucker, W. Edwards Deming, and Tom Peters have stated that American managers are functionally illiterate when it comes to using quantitative operating data. Most recently, Drucker was quoted in the *Wall Street Journal* (Dec. 1, 1992, p. A1): "Few executives yet know how to ask: What information do I need for my job? When do I need it? And from whom should I be getting it?"

If we exclude manufacturing and sales, I tend to agree with the illiteracy charge. My experience with staff departments has shown that they are generally the least skilled in numbers related to operational performance. Given this certain-to-be controversial indictment, it is not surprising that metrics are frequently neglected or misused in benchmarking. When they are included, it is often as an afterthought. In some cases, a few questions requiring numeric answers are thrown in at the end of the list. Their relevance is not always apparent; often they have none. The numeric questions frequently are not well connected to the process data. The end result is that a few tables or graphs are presented with references to certain parts of the process discussion but with no true causal or correlational evidence to support their inclusion.

A number of factors account for this neglect: the focus on activity, the lack of numeric analysis skills, the deficient understanding of the full value of objective data, the regarding of staff work as an expense rather than as a value, and a misconception of how to develop and use numbers to inform, motivate, and reward performance. If staff managers would shift their view from administering their function to adding value to the enterprise, they would surely seek out methods for measuring the value generated. In effect, everyone from the manager down is, or should be, charged with managing the organization's assets.

Asset Management and Measurement

Starting your benchmarking investigation with the value-adding perspective spawns new insights regarding your approach and methods and consequently enriches your results. Using asset management as a launching point leads you to consider how people and systems relate in carrying out organizational processes. That relationship is what benchmarking seeks to uncover. Figure 3.1 shows the arrangement of assets and processes and how they lead to measurable changes in performance. The amount or degree of the changes referred to is measured in cost, time, quantity, quality, and human reactions. Figure 3.2 is a matrix that illustrates the placement of those measures across

Figure 3.1. From Assets Through Processes
to Value Added: Steps in the Model.

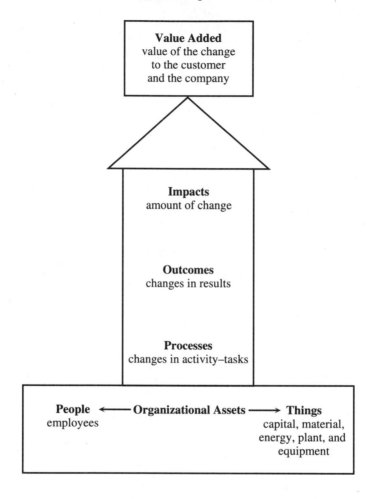

the process-to-value array. You can cost changes in terms of processes–outcomes–impacts and certainly of value added. Likewise, you can often apply time, quantity, quality, and human reaction metrics to changes in processes, outcomes, impacts, and value added.

The terminology and foundation of the asset-value interaction were introduced in the discussion of the value-adding

Figure 3.2. Measurement Matrix.

Actions

	Processes	Outcomes	Impacts	Value
Cost				
Time				
Quantity				
Quality				
Human Reaction				

Indices

chain in Chapter One. Here I provide graphic examples of how they relate to each other. By viewing any function from this bottom-up perspective, the benchmark team is led to consider the details that make the processes work. These are the underlying elements that hold the potential for improvement. When people don't start from this organic level, they often produce a result that is of superficial value.

Organic Measurement of Organizational Phenemona

The value-adding method is a more organic approach than the traditional financial accounting system. *Organic* is a term commonly used in the physical and biological sciences rather than in business. Let me explain how it applies in the organizational milieu. Engineering is organic work. It is concerned with how machines or systems function. Accounting is a mathematical discipline that is applied to the work. It counts what is happening, but it explains only a few relationships. Each method has its purpose. If you want to know how an automobile works, you don't ask an accountant. Accounting can tell you things like the car's fuel consumption rate. An accountant can also show you how that rate is changing over time. Engineering can take those data and look at the car's carburetor, spark plugs, or timing to learn why fuel consumption is increasing. When you approach benchmarking from an asset-management, value-adding viewpoint, you begin to understand how the corporate organism is functioning and where the problems or opportunities lie. In this example, the automobile is the organization and the owner/driver is the customer.

The value-adding method of measuring organizational phenomena uses many of the same variables that financial and managerial accountants use. Since the organizational field is finite, managerial measurement differs simply in how you arrange your metrics. Think of it in terms of cooking. The cuisine of any given country has a limited number of ingredients. Each cook just mixes them differently to achieve different results. The same is true for value-adding measurement. We mix variables differently and view them on a tactical level. Here we can look at other relationships. We want to know *why* and *how* as well as *what*. For example, how does running a process in a particular way affect outcomes that have an impact on other departments and on the ultimate customer? Why does your benchmark partner sequence the process the way it does?

Leibfried and McNair (1992, pp. 168–169) offer a short list of strategic and tactical-level productivity, quality, and service measures for staff operations that the Saratoga Institute has adapted and added to. Table 3.1 displays some of their measures incorporated with others and modified for our purposes.

As asset managers we are all obliged to wring the most out of assets under our control — within ethical and legal limits, of course. In order to obtain the best output-to-input ratios we need data: quantitative, objective, relevant data. I had one client who for years had been generating roughly two pounds of reports each month on his operation. When I looked through them, I suggested he had two choices: dump them or severely constrict and refocus the reporting. He had a mountain of data on oper-

Table 3.1. Staff Measures.

Staff Productivity
- Output divided by headcount
- Cost per unit of service produced
- Service output divided by resource input
- Value added per employee
- Items processed per employee hour
- Nonvalue-added costs

Staff Quality
- Error rates
- Percentage of back orders
- Percentage of on-time delivery
- Percentage of outputs reworked
- Forecast accuracy
- Process cycle time

Staff Service
- Number of customer complaints
- Mean time to repair
- Mean time to fill requests
- Percentage of work accepted
- Customer satisfaction ratings
- Mean time to respond

ating volumes, such as number of items processed. What was missing was an explanation of the *value* of his reports. They showed only activity; hence, expense. Every month he was showing the organization that he was spending a lot of time, money, and resources, but he never reported any value added. In the eyes of his top management, he was an expense center, not an asset manager. When we finished the project we had reduced his reporting to about a dozen items on as many pages, complete with a narrative explanation of trends and value added. After top management saw this, they began to view him as someone who shared their interests and values.

Reversing the View

Rather than developing a list of variables that can be used to explain your operation, focus on the other end of the process. Ask yourself, what are the key cost, time, quantity, quality, and human issues that you need to understand to manage and improve your function. In other words, where do you want to add value? Value can be added at the human level, with employees and customers; at the production level, in terms of quality, productivity, or service; or at the financial level, for return on investment, return on assets or equity, or market share. By turning the picture around you focus on why you are there. Your job is not to manage some activity. Your responsibility as an asset manager is to achieve results. Those results fall into the categories identified above. By looking at the situation from this end you avoid being seduced into monitoring activity.

Ceteris Paribus . . .

In functions that traditionally have done little to measure their operation, there is always some degree of resistance. Every imaginable roadblock is set up by people who are fearful of how the measures will be used. While their fears need to be acknowledged, you can't let them stop you. The most common objection that is brought up revolves around the interval between making an intervention and measuring the result. A lot can happen during that time, therefore, the protesters claim, it is virtually impossible to show any type of cause-and-effect relationship between the action and the distant result. The best and only effective way to counteract this argument is to operate from the standpoint that the future must always be dealt with under ceteris paribus conditions. This is a Latin term meaning "other things being equal," frequently used in scientific experiments. The only way we can predict or project the value of a current action on a future outcome is to presume ceteris paribus. We know that this will not be the case, but if we tried to hypothesize all possible scenarios we would never act.

    Despite the obvious logic for taking a ceteris paribus position, some managers still have problems accepting it. One staff department of a major insurance company has always been uncomfortable with ceteris paribus. As a result, they will accept only the simplest and most obvious measures. This tends to focus them on the monitoring of activities, which offers less potential value.

    Business managers make assumptions in every projection. It is the only way anyone can project. When you develop your budget you say, in effect, if market costs do not change dramatically this is what it will cost us to operate. You also assume that there will be no additional responsibilities added to your unit during the budget period. Furthermore, your operating beliefs are that the people who have an impact on your budget will act in accordance with a given set of behaviors. Of course, you know from experience that many of your assumptions will fail to come true. Some will hurt your projection and some will help, but if you did not make ceteris paribus assumptions you would not be able to say anything about the future.

The Value Chain

Benchmarking is about studying processes for the purpose of adding value. It is easier to make the leap from process to value if you know what and where the stepping stones are. If you look at both Figures 3.1 and 3.2 you will see two different expressions of the same idea. The following describes the linkage.

Processes

Process measurement deals principally with activity rather than with outcomes. The assumption is that if you clean up the process, the outcomes will improve. Process measures focus on error or defect rates and cycle times — the time it takes to complete one step in the process or the entire process. There is nothing mysterious about measuring errors or cycle times, as many quality programs have shown. But measurement for the sake of measurement is a waste. We have to learn what to measure. What is worth measuring to discover a traceable effect on the organization or the customer? In Typically Ltd., several measurable processes and outcomes could be traced to value added. If one staff department improves its process metrics, it will affect the processes and therefore the outcomes of other departments. If shipping at Typically Ltd. receives clear orders from sales, shipment cycle time and error rate should improve. Shipping can then send better data sooner to accounting and customer service, thereby improving the outputs of both those units, and so on through the system.

In manufacturing, process variables have long been studied as a path to reducing unit costs. Yet, for the reasons mentioned above, a mythology has developed in staff functions that you can't or shouldn't measure staff processes. Many people believe that even if they knew error rates or cycle times, the knowledge would not make any difference because they are dealing with an invisible service, not a visible product. One middle manager told me, "It won't make a difference because the system won't change." This frustration is typical of many people in the trenches, and with good reason. Many inefficient systems and processes don't change because management doesn't experience the inefficiency every day as the workers do. The key to selling change is to show how it would add value at the impact level. The problem is, most people don't know how to trace the changes in their processes to a value-added result for the organization or the customer because they tend to skip the outcome step. They have told themselves that a great many things happen between the process and the impact; therefore, the ultimate effect will be invisible and incalculable. The first part of that argument is true, but the second is not.

In business, we are not dealing with laboratory research. We cannot control for all variables and therefore be able to prove something at the .05 level of statistical significance. Scientists and theoreticians need to do that. Business managers can't do it and don't need to. This uncontrollability argument is a smoke screen put up by people who don't want to do the measuring. It is purely an excuse. A mountain of evidence exists within the many organizations where the Saratoga Institute has worked, demonstrating that solid measures of value added have been created for many staff functions.

A process fixation hides within the psyches of many staff managers and goes all the way up to the vice-presidential levels. I was doing a training session on value management for a Fortune 100 company when this trait burst out in living color. The executive vice president (EVP) kept suggesting to the senior vice president (SVP) that he turn over this or that process function to someone in accounting. He pointed out that accountants do this work all the time and could probably gain some economies of scale by integrating it into their work systems. The EVP went on to say that if he got rid of this stuff, the SVP's professional staff could spend more time really adding value instead of burying themselves in administrivia. The SVP repeatedly claimed he couldn't and offered some clearly spurious reasons. It turned out that the SVP did not know how to add value through his function—but he sure knew how to process paper and he was very comfortable overseeing it.

An improvement in error rates or cycle times must have value if the function itself has any value. The only issues are, Where is the value and how much is there? We have already established that staff functions exist because they add some value somewhere; we simply have to trace the value path. If you shorten the time to do something, it should have an effect on your customers' work. Obviously, they receive your product sooner, which means they can start their process sooner; then their customers receive their product sooner, and so on until—all things being equal—the ultimate customer is served faster.

There are two potential values here. One assumes that the customer would like the product (or service) faster. If the customer received it sooner, that should improve customer relations. This would make subsequent transactions easier and give your organization a competitive edge. This is what benchmarking sets out to do in the value-planning step that we will discuss in the next chapter. If time is not an issue with your customer, then there is no point in benchmarking the process for the purpose of improving cycle time. Instead, you might look at reduction of error rates. Track that and see whether improving it would add value for the customer.

The second point is the issue of other things being equal, which was addressed earlier. This is the second self-imposed barrier to measuring process. This is the classic argument of trainers who don't want to measure the effects of their work. They claim, and rightly so, that between the time they train and when some impact can be recorded, many other events can affect the outcomes. The answer to that is, So what? Rather than lament what supposedly cannot be done, a trainer can show that someone obtained a new skill, which can be proven by testing during or at the end of the course. If the skill did not cause subsequent outcomes to change in the workplace, then we have isolated another organizational problem. Now we can attack that problem and solve it.

The only way you can measure something is to freeze the world for a moment and say, all other things being equal, this is what would happen. This is exactly what we do with projections of sales or manufacturing. We set conditions (freeze the world) and say, If these prevail, and if we follow our plan, then we should make or sell X number of units. After the fact we look at the results and ask ourselves what caused them. Was it a function of what we did or did something unforeseen happen? We try to learn from that, adjust our approach and go on. Remember what Udo Schulz said: progress, not perfection.

The fact is, when you pull the engine apart, you can learn the source of the problem, but as long as you tell yourself there are so many reasons for increased fuel consumption that you will never find the cause, you never will. And you will continue to spend more money on gasoline. The mystery of effective performance is not a function of complexity; it is a result of fuzzy thinking or indolence.

Outcomes

Assuming we find an improvement in processes, we can look at outcomes and see what is there. Manufacturing outcomes deal with unit cost and quantity of product manufactured. Improvements in manufacturing processes shorten time to ship. Reduction of product defects, or improvement in quality, leads to lower product cost and less service expense. The interaction of cost, time, quantity, and quality becomes obvious. Sales outcomes deal with gross revenue from sales, sales margins, number of products sold, and selling costs. Improvement in sales processes, not only face-to-face selling skills but also something such as more efficient calling routes, can have an effect on quantity sold and cost of sales. These are simple examples, but you can see how they apply to other aspects of production and sales. Much more complex and penetrating measures can be taken. You just have to dig a little deeper.

How does improving the outcome apply in staff functions? There is little fundamental difference between processing paper in accounting or purchasing and producing products in manufacturing, applicants in recruiting, or reports in data operations. All processes run according to the same general rules of input–throughput–output. Only the labels on the items differ. Being forced to acknowledge that, the naysayers set out the next mythical roadblock, so-called professional work. They claim that professionals don't do routine, continuous process work. That is somewhat true, although not as true as these people prefer to think. Simply stated, it is a matter of looking at practices as well as processes. The thesaurus offers manners, habits, and customs as primary synonyms for practices. For processes, it lists operations or procedures. These subtle differences clear a path around the professionalism barrier. Where there is the will, we have found the way. It's inescapable.

Benchmarkers can study the processing of accounting, staffing, information services, and other staff functions to find ways to reduce errors and shorten cycle time. The benchmark project will be able to trace the improvements in cost and quantity outcomes. The question that you are now familiar with is, Is this the best opportunity to obtain an outcome value now? If not, check another process for opportunity.

Let's return to the professional work question. I spent seven years in the banking business. The myth there was that the mental process of making a loan decision was something mystical. Legend had it that making loan decisions was a judgment call that could not be subjected to process analysis. Nothing could be further from the truth. Bankers disproved their own theory when they went to formula installment lending. Applicants answered seven to ten questions, giving responses on a scale. The points were added up and the results determined whether they did or did not qualify for a loan. In more complex commercial lending, the customer applies for a loan by filling out innumerable forms. These give financial and personal history back through a minimum of three previous incarnations. Bankers would like you to believe that the decision process is something mystical. Wrong! The facts are that lending is very structured. Lending is based on the 5C's: character, collateral, capacity, capital, and credit. Loans aren't made to everyone who walks in off the street. You know what your chances are of getting a loan from a bank where you don't have a history as a customer. Loan officers usually know their customers except when management strips the authority for lending out of the branch and sets up central loan committees, an example of a practice rather than a process. (This committee structure is known as "how to hide the blame.") In either case, the forms are scanned, ratios calculated, and decisions generated with very little room for error.

So how do you improve the thought process? Try training. Teach lenders how to read financial statements better and faster. How do you know they can do it? Try testing. It is clear that a trained loan officer can dig certain information out of a financial document that an untrained one can't. That skill can be tested. Go through each of the forms and look for ways to make them easier to fill out, easier to interpret, and more useful. Lending forms haven't changed in fifty years so they can't be that unfathomable.

The same principles of work management apply to being a professional accountant, recruiter, programmer, facilities engineer, or whatever. The only variant is that you apply them in slightly different ways in each situation. In the end we are faced with the task of defining and codifying a best practice for managing professional work in a given function. Think in terms of how this practice affects the customer. If we did it differently, would the new way add value?

Impacts

The impact question is answered by describing the difference an improvement in a process made to an outcome. When a product or service cost is reduced, or the time to deliver or respond to a call for customer service is shortened, what difference does it make?

Take the case of customer service. What are the customer's expectations? Which are being realized? What can be done to improve customer satisfaction with our professional services?

We may be able to change a process or practice so as to speed up the service, reduce the cost of delivering the service, and thereby gain an edge in customer satisfaction. That is a value-adding impact. If those things don't make a difference to the customer, then there has been a neutral impact. Something happened, but the customer doesn't care.

Would you consider selling to be a professional service or an administrative process? The sales force of Ball Seed Company, a *Best Practice Report* (Saratoga Institute, 1992) company, has long enjoyed a reputation for providing good customer service. It was so good that when the company benchmarked it, they decided that their service level was a competitive advantage in the wholesale flower and seed business. To make it even better, they equipped their field salespeople with small computers that could access Ball's inventories and incoming order status and give the customer shipping dates on the spot. This further separated them from the competition. The impact of the automation investment was improved customer service. The value added was that sales and market share increased.

In Ball's case, the process of selling the customer was changed by the introduction of the use of computers by salespeople to inform the customer on the spot—the outcome. The primary impact was an improved selling situation. It defined in specific terms what we expect to happen or what did happen. Other impacts are the reinforced image of Ball as the best service company in the business and probably an improved relationship between the salesperson and the buyer. These are answers to the question, If we use computers, what difference will it make? Impact is the penultimate goal. Customer satisfaction leading to increased sales is the ultimate goal. If the on-the-spot information did not facilitate the sale, then we had a neutral impact. In this case it did improve the ratio of calls to sales, and the dollar value of the additional sales is the return on the investment—the value added.

Value-Adding Linkage

The linkage from processes or practices through outcomes to impacts and value added is straightforward. Measurement can occur at each step beginning with the process or practice, but without applying metrics in the beginning there is no way to know where to start. Metrics must be connected to the process or practice. This is the verification procedure that tells you where you stand. Metrics are needed to confirm a best practice with a potential benchmarking partner. Some companies receive a lot of publicity. Yet, when you contact them and ask how they measure their effectiveness you often find very vague references to a poorly defined outcome. Furthermore, when you go one step further to ask what effect the outcomes are having on the organization or the customer, you might discover that they don't know. Finally, measures are needed to monitor the results of the benchmarking project. Were things changed? Did it make the improvements predicted? Was there added value? If so, how much? Figure 3.3 provides sample applications of the process–outcome–impact–value-added chain.

Examining the linkage shows clearly how you can look at a process or practice and track the potential value through outcomes and impacts. Figure 3.3 is a linear example. In practice, one process improvement may produce more than one outcome and may lead to several impacts with a number of added values. Cost, time, quantity, quality, and human reaction measures can be applied throughout the chain. Take an example from Figure 3.3:

> *Process:* A change in service-call routing may mean fewer miles driven and less gas consumed in the trip process. Less time would be spent en route as well.
>
> *Outcomes:* A few of the outcomes broadly described as increased efficiency would be money saved on fuel and vehicle maintenance. The service person is also less fatigued since he or she spends less time traveling.
>
> *Impact:* This outcome could lead to the impact (difference between old and new outcomes) of more calls per service agent. It probably also makes for higher quality calls since the person is less fatigued.
>
> *Value:* These impacts mean more productivity, culminating in the value added of more revenue generated by each agent. As a result of the benchmarking-driven

Figure 3.3. Samples of Value Added from Benchmarking.

Process/Practice →	Outcome →	Impact →	Value Added
Change service-call routing	Increased efficiency	More calls per service agent	Service revenue increase
Speed up service dispatching	Faster response to customer	More satisfied customers	Fewer lost customers
Decrease service recall rate	Fewer service calls	More calls per service person	Reduced service cost
Design out process flaws	Fewer product defects	Less rework	Lower product cost
Simplify hiring process	Shortened time to hire	Jobs filled sooner	Less overtime/fewer temps
Upgrade training capability	Increased return on investment from training	Higher productivity	Lower product cost
Survey information interests	Improved employee communication	Better morale/less turnover	Retention savings
Reduce work-process steps	More efficient work flow	Faster cycle time/delivery	More competitive
Centralize hiring	Lower agency rates	Lower hiring cost	Reduced operating expense
Accelerate sales reports	Earlier receipt of sales data	Sales information more useful	More sales per person
Redistribute work load	Reduced employee stress	Less absenteeism	Reduced sick leave expense
Improve maintenance	Cleaner, safer facilities	Fewer accidents	Less worker compensation cost
Write error-free software	Faster record creation	More records per hour	Lower record-keeping cost

changes in service call routing, the company has obtained reductions in service costs and increases in revenue from service.

There are other values that we can check out. These could include greater customer satisfaction because of service provided by a less fatigued, unhurried agent. If service personnel are less stressed, their absenteeism will decrease, claims against the employee health program may drop, and even turnover might improve. The dollar value of these types of changes can also be calculated. Even though many top executives genuinely care about the employees, they still like to see dollar returns on their investments in benchmarking.

Conclusion

Measurement of any work process or practice is more than possible. It is imperative. It applies in both routinized process work and in individual professional practices. Whether we are talking about a benchmarking project or just tending to day-to-day management, without numbers we don't really know what we are doing. If managers do not know how much their product/ service costs, how long it takes to deliver, how much is being delivered, and how the end result matches the customers' requirements, I have only one question: What do they think they are managing? Without metrics, managers are only caretakers. They are administrators of processes.

Benchmarking is about adding value through process investigation and improvement. We seek to add value, not just understand a process better. It is more than knowing the what or the how-to of a best practice. To make lasting change we need to know why people do what they do and we need to see hard evidence (metrics) that this is a cost-effective way to do it. Unfortunately, some CEOs mistakenly think they can run large organizations in a world-class manner with managers who don't measure their work. The administrative areas, which encompass everything except manufacturing, R&D, and direct sales, house a large portion of the employees and most of the processes of the organization. To allow this group to run without any sense of how their productivity, quality, or service compares to the competition is sheer folly.

All employees must become asset managers if businesses are to compete in today's marketplace. They should use the asset-to-value chain as the basis for managing the organization's human, material, capital, energy, plant, and equipment assets. This understanding will help them plan the investment of their assets in a manner that will yield the greatest return.

Those who claim that the world is too dynamic and complex to measure change must be reminded of two words: ceteris paribus. Nothing is totally predictable, but everything is projectable. We can say, and we do presume every day, that other things being equal, this is what should result from our actions. We cannot allow the naysayers to frustrate the good intentions and honest efforts of our people.

Measurement applies all along the route, from analyzing a practice or process to calculating the value added by the impact. Benchmarkers need measurement for at least four reasons:

1. To know where they stand at the beginning
2. To decide if a given process improvement might add value and how much value it might add
3. To qualify potential benchmark partners
4. To monitor and evaluate the results of the benchmarking effort

One of the best features of benchmarking is that it generates external data that become a comparative indicator of performance. This eliminates the ability of internal people to develop measures that protect themselves and mislead the organization. The relevant numbers that can be generated from benchmarking tell the true story of competitiveness.

4

Value Planning: Selecting and Launching the Right Project

The purpose of benchmarking is to add value, that is, to improve the company's competitive position. To add value, the benchmark team needs to build a chain from the staff department process they are planning to improve, through their internal customers' processes and outcomes, culminating in the potential value added for the external customer. Value should be defined as a measurable gain in quality, productivity, or service such that the company gains advantage in the marketplace.

The first step in a benchmarking venture is planning. I insist on calling it value planning so that the value driver is always up front. The value-planning phase includes five activities:

1. Identifying potential value-creation opportunities within staff functions
2. Comparing the value potential of each function for internal and external effects
3. Selecting the benchmark target(s) that will yield greatest return on effort
4. Organizing and training the benchmarking project players
5. Locating, contacting, and qualifying benchmarking partners

Too often projects are launched with unclear, incomplete, or internally disputed goals. Rather than having a focused idea of where they are going and why they must get there, managers use benchmarking as a knee-jerk reaction to pressure from some direction.

Because benchmarking is so new, many people have had little or no experience with it. Consequently, they don't know where to start. They have heard that it is a way to identify and fix problems or to exploit opportunities by gathering data from people who know how to do something well and copying them. Typically, a small group of people will get together and agree that they would like to benchmark one or several processes to make them work better. The first questions to ask are, What do we mean by better? Would we know it if we saw it? What would better look like? Would something be faster or slower, cost less, yield more, have fewer defects, create happier employees or more satisfied customers, and if it did, how much better would we expect the process to be? Finally, if we were able to achieve that improvement, what would it be worth? And to whom — you, the company, your customers, employees, the stockholders, the community?

An unfocused, poorly directed effort such as this would likely happen at Typically Ltd. The procurement manager has heard about benchmarking at a conference. Unless he spends some time getting educated, the chances of his carrying out an effective benchmarking project are slim.

American businesses must become more scientific in allocating their resources to projects that have big paybacks. We are never going to catch the competition with our present approach. The degree of sloppiness in our thinking is appalling at times. On one occasion the Saratoga Institute was called in to provide a process for measuring the strategic value of a company's human assets. The job had to be done in one week! Despite our best attempts to wring a definition out of the group who hired us, we left with a very vague target. Working day and night for a week we delivered a state-of-the-art system for measuring the strategic performance of human assets. Of course, when we presented the product a week later the client group was dissatisfied. It was at that point that they admitted they did not know what they had in mind. Within three months the group driving the project was disbanded.

Efficient Benchmarking

If we are going to commit resources to a benchmarking project we should ensure that the process is efficient. It helps to have a structure (such as the four-step model in Figure 2.3) around which to plan. Experienced benchmarkers have found that without one they waste a lot of everyone's time and their results are seldom what they hope for. After designing your structure you will want to have a process for moving quickly into the project with the full knowledge and support of all parties. Management is becoming less tolerant of expenditures for projects that have not been thoroughly thought-out.

It is important to identify quickly the critical success factors, or CSFs. These are the issues that have the greatest potential impact on organizational performance. The staff managers at Typically Ltd. should think about their CSFs from the viewpoint of how they might be improved to affect market share. They can use these questions to identify the CSFs within their departments:

1. What is the highest value-potential factor in our function? That is, what would be the outcome that would most help our organization achieve its mission?
2. Is the greatest value to be found in improving quality, productivity, or service?
3. Which processes are most critical in achieving that value?
4. Which processes currently show the greatest room for improvement?
5. Which processes might be the easiest to fix?
6. Will the final competitive advantage for the company come from an increase in revenue, a reduction in operating expense, or an improvement in customer satisfaction?

There are four value levels within a benchmarking project's organization: *target function, process area, activities,* and *value outcomes.* Exhibit 4.1 is a sample of how these levels are used to examine a particular function. Each level moves you from a general area to a more specific issue.

Exhibit 4.1. Value Levels.

Level 1. Target Function: Staffing

Level 2. Process Area: College recruiting

Level 3. Activities: *Contact points:* placement office, faculty, student groups
Interviewing roles: recruiting staff, line managers
Offer process: visit to company, who makes offer, when is it made
General relations: research grants, reciprocal visiting, sponsorships

Level 4. Value Outcomes: Costs, time, offer reject reasons, quality of hires

---

Target Function

Targeting the function is the broadest level and is usually the easiest to do. Once in a while, benchmark projects are launched simply because someone is curious. This is often the case the first time a company decides to benchmark. There are so many opportunities for making improvements in organizations that you could throw a dart at a wall full of processes and always hit something worthwhile. At that point, the first value judgment is generally made. Someone usually asks and answers the questions above, which leads them to the rationale for spending their time on one process rather than on another. On that basis, the decision is made to go after a given function because there is more, or at least as much, opportunity to add value there than somewhere else.

Process Area

The process area is one of the many responsibilities that fall within the target function. If accounting were the target function, accounts payable could be the process area. Other process areas include the various subdivisions of accounting, such as accounts receivable, cost accounting, tax, and payroll. If information systems was the target, the process area could be within data operations, systems development, or systems maintenance.

The scope of the project is set at this point. Will you benchmark the whole function or just one process? The decision is based on the potential value. How bad are things? Conversely, how much better could/should they be? Are major across-the-board improvements called for or do you just need to tweak one area?

As you move down through levels you need to involve more people who work in those areas. They have the best knowledge of process and system flows because they have to work with them every day. This is the point where you need to document the process, to confirm your preliminary decision. The people who work the process can create a flow chart to identify the inputs, the process flow, the activities at each step, the outputs, and the measures of time, quantity, and cost.

Activities

Within the process there are several subdivisions. These are the tasks and activities that are carried out to fulfill the process. For example, you would divide college recruiting, a division of the employment process, into the following activities (also displayed in Exhibit 4.1):

1. Contact points
   - College placement office: how do we work with them?
   - Faculty: what role do they play?
   - Student groups: what clubs should we meet with, such as marketing, engineering?
2. Interviewing roles
   - Recruiting staff: preparation, logistics.
   - Line managers: what level and how many participate?
3. Offer process
   - Visit to the company.
   - Who makes the offer?
   - At what point is it made?
4. General relations
   - Research grants.
   - Class visits to company.
   - Company speakers on campus.
   - Company sponsored campus events.

These are a few of the many issues a company must address in the process of college recruiting.

Value Outcomes

The last level is the outcome or result. Outcome values are both quantitative and qualitative. They include costs of hiring, time spent by various individuals, reasons for offers being rejected, and quality of hires. This level is the proof of the effectiveness of the process. Quite often people will search out benchmark partners, go through the project with them, develop data, and still not be able to determine which factors in the list of activities had an effect on the outcome. In short, benchmarking as they practiced it was an interesting waste of time. There is a natural connection between the four levels. To obtain a useful result, you must take care to maintain the flow through the levels as you progress. If you do, when you finish the job you will have developed a process through which you can continually add value.

Identifying the Value To Be Added

The basic question is simple yet penetrating: How much value would be added if you improved productivity, quality, or service in this case? Most people cannot answer that question at first; but with a little training in quantitative evaluation methodology and a few examples of value added, they begin to see that a given improvement can be traced to a gain in money, time, quantity, quality, or human reaction. Typically Ltd. staff managers would look at the processes they brought up in the meeting and try to establish a value path. What is the effect of timelines or accuracy improvement on their internal customers' processes? How would that improvement enhance their outcomes? What effect would internal improvement have on the outside customer? Would this help recapture market share?

There is a great deal of intuitive, experiential knowledge lodged in the subconscious of most businesspeople. They just lack a way of thinking that opens the door and lets it out. Once they begin to think about an issue, they instinctively grasp that if they make an improvement, the company will either earn money or save money. The improvement might save time, which can be valued in terms of the cost of overtime or shortened training periods or faster shipments, all of which have a calculable value. It could allow them to do more in the same amount of time, which is also a quantifiable productivity gain. It probably would decrease errors or product defects, the results of which would create a measurable benefit. Finally, all things being equal, the improvement could enhance customer service or reclaim a formerly unhappy customer, thereby producing a competitive edge or saving the cost of capturing a replacement customer. When you begin to think of value in this simple way it becomes an easy exercise. As you add up the value achieved, all things being equal, you will have a measurable improvement in the business on either the revenue or the expense side. Later in this chapter we will look at a list of the types of values that can be obtained through benchmarking.

It is clear that the opportunities for significant improvement are endless. To focus your benchmarking projects on the most fruitful areas, you should conduct a value analysis before any other steps are taken. This will ensure the best return on your investment.

Value Planning

Value planning involves five distinct activities. These are discussed in the sections following.

1. Identifying Opportunities for Potential Value Creation Within Staff Functions

Value is everywhere just waiting to be found. We have only to look for it. Visualize the organization chart and the financial statements side by side. On one side are the standard functions: production, sales, R&D, finance, administration. On the other are the income statement and the balance sheet with their traditional ratios. Merge them in your mind. This exercise should lead you to strategic-level problems and opportunities for increasing revenues and/or reducing expenses within each of the functional business units. The prime question is, what can you do to improve profitability and increase market share? Next, apply managerial accounting measures to each function's departmental subdivisions. These tactical-level measures let you see where the opportunities lie. You make improvements in the strategic corporate performance measures by uncovering opportunity within the processes and systems of each business unit. The following is a short list of typical target areas for staff value-adding benchmarking:

Internal customer satisfaction
Service (product) quality
  and design
Training program effectiveness
Accounts receivable and
  payable
Facilities maintenance pro-
  cedures
Real estate management
Policies and rules in any area

Service call outcomes
Hiring strategy
Telecommunications efficiency
Information processing costs
Safety/security levels
Procurement methods
Administrative/corporate
  services

Every business unit has within it people, processes, technology, and structure variables that are either working for or against the goals of the organization. Businesses are social systems that should be constructed around a shared set of goals. Most of the time there is a sense of common purpose, but sometimes this commonality is weakened, usually by something management does. Despite these lapses, only in the worst cases do we find that people are consciously working against the best interests of the organization. In most instances, problems arise because processes are inefficient, technology is not effectively deployed, or organizational systems are counterproductive. The question is, how would value be added if we changed *this* system or *this* process?

On the revenue-generating side are sales and service activities that affect revenue directly or indirectly. Also located here are functions such as research and development. Although some might claim that R&D is an expense, it seems to me that without new and improved products to sell and service there will be no revenue. People would also like to think that advertising and public relations have a positive effect on the ability to make sales. These functions are supposed to position the company and its products in ways that make selling easier. Most people would list training as an expense. I put it on the investment side with R&D. If training is not directly helping to increase revenue, then its funding ought to be reconsidered. I grant that all those activities cost money, but what doesn't? The issue of revenue generation is not whether money was spent on it, but whether the positive effect of that investment on sales or service improvements can be found.

On the expense side, managers usually list the staff departments. Most companies treat them as necessary evils, at best. But staff departments can — and should — be run as value generators. The notion that weds staff to overhead is out-of-date. Consider why you have staff functions. Do you hire people in those areas because you just want to spend money, or do you hire them because they add some type of value? The answer is obvious. Staff adds value, provided it works with the vision of that value. Value comes in two flavors: increased revenue and decreased expense. Granted, in some companies accounting, facilities, human resources, information services, and the rest are considered only process centers that do not add value. On the other hand, the Saratoga Institute has worked with hundreds of companies, profit and not-for-profit, where those groups are expected to add value in measurable terms, and they do. It is a matter of getting what you expect.

It should be clear that value-adding opportunities can be found within product design and marketing, sales and service processes, corporate imaging, procurement, financial services, human resources and facilities management, and information service products. The key to locating the opportunity is to delve deeply into each task or process and ask the question, how would it add value if we improved this? Now, you begin to see that benchmarking is not rocket science or brain surgery. It is just logical, painstaking work.

2. Comparing the Value Potential of Each Opportunity for Internal and External Effects

In Figure 3.2, I presented an example (the Measurement Matrix) of the procedure for identifying where the greatest value opportunity lies. Exhibit 4.2 lists many examples of activities and outcomes adapted from Sloma (1980), Fitz-enz (1984), Leibfried and McNair (1992), and other sources. These are just a small fraction of the processes, practices, and outcomes that could be investigated to identify significant value-adding opportunities. Data on these types of measures can be found through a wide variety of sources. Principal examples are the following:

- Trade and professional associations
- Research centers such as the Electric Power Research Institute
- American Productivity and Quality Center
- American Management Association
- American Society for Quality Control
- Saratoga Institute
- Strategic Planning Institute
- Washington Researchers

There is an inherent synergy among many of the seventy-plus factors in the lists contained in Figures 3.1 and 4.2. For example, improving the service recall rate not only cuts the cost of service, which indirectly affects the cost of the product, but also makes customers more satisfied with the organization's service. Reducing lead time on purchases cuts inventory costs, which reduces product cost. Filling jobs faster cuts overtime costs and improves customer satisfaction because someone is on the job to help them. Having timely and accurate data not only makes selling easier, but also enhances the company's reputation as a knowledgeable and customer-focused organization. The key question is, where is the greatest value to be obtained? How much value would be added if you benchmarked and improved this outcome versus another? Time and resources are precious commodities today. You want to use them as cost effectively as possible.

Exhibit 4.2. Activities and Outcomes for Benchmarking.

MIS Management

EDP/MIS costs divided by sales
Percentage of jobs completed on time
Overtime costs
Backlog hours
Value of reports (use paired
    comparison)

Financial Management

Aging of receivables
Cash balances
Percentage of budget variances over
    X percent
Accuracy of cost accounting procedures
Percentage of tax filings on time

Human Resource Management

Time to fill jobs
Cost per hire
Cost/errors in payroll and benefit
    processing
Absenteeism/turnover rates and costs
Pay/benefits as percentage of operating
    expense

Employee Development

Cost of training per trainee hour
Time to design and deliver new
    training
Value of training programs
Number of people trained
Value of succession planning system

Miscellaneous Internal Services

Usage rates/service levels of media
    centers
Service unit expense levels of each
    function
Project and request response time
Internal customer satisfaction level

Customer Service Management

Mean time to response
Mean time to repair
Service unit cost
Customer satisfaction level

Facilities Management

Work order turnaround time
Percentage of solid waste recycled
Telecommunications usage and cost
Square footage used per person
Maintenance of comfort levels
    (complaints)

Safety and Security Management

Accident rates
Lost time level
Workers compensation costs
Security incident rates
Employee satisfaction survey
    responses

Marketing Management

Marketing costs per sales revenue
Advertising costs per sales revenue
Distribution costs
Sales administration costs
New products introduced

Purchasing Management

Average cost to process a requisition
Average lead time to purchase
On-time delivery rate
Percentage of purchases rejected
Inventory as a percentage of production

3. Selecting the Benchmark Target(s)
That Will Yield the Greatest Return on Effort

When you finish steps one and two, you will have the answer to step three. It is now a matter of deciding on which of the many possible targets you want to focus your resources. Here are some thoughts that may help you make that decision.

It is hard to go wrong if you start from the back and work forward. Many people start with a process and work toward the improvement. You have gone the other way. You have asked how (and how much) value would be added if you tackled one or another of the many process areas. Remember, value is ultimately what the customer says it is. You may have identified a process that could stand some major improvement. From an internal standpoint, I am certain you are right. The point to consider then is, what impact will this improvement have on your customers?

If you can trace the internal value added to its impact, as we did at the beginning of this chapter, it will narrow the range of choices. From the perspective of market position, is your company trying to establish itself as a leader in price, quality, service, delivery, flexibility, responsiveness, or what? What is its vision of itself? You need to have a clear vision of your organization so that you can create or dominate a market niche, in order to stand out or to be remembered. You can be part of a major corporation that is known worldwide for its uniqueness, but you can also achieve market recognition if you are a small firm. Let me use my company as an example.

In the late 1970s, I set out to establish the Saratoga Institute as *the* source for quantitative data related to human resources. My vision of the institute was clear: when anyone thought about how their organization compared to others in hiring, paying, benefits, training, retention, and other such matters, I wanted them to think first and only of the Saratoga Institute as a data source. We resisted temptations to take work in other areas because if we did, our image would be clouded. It cost us money for many years. But today, in more than thirty countries around the world, if you ask about operating data on human resources, you will be referred to only one place. The major consulting companies buy our services and refer us to their clients. All the trade associations direct their members toward us. Every decision we make about improving our operation, our revenue, or our market position is driven by the "source" criterion. Along the way my original vision of our purpose expanded to take in all staff functions, but it never changed from being an information source to something more fragmented or ambiguous.

If you are going to spend resources on benchmarking, not to mention on everything else you do, you want to be certain that the result will strengthen your market position. The question that immediately comes up when I make that statement is, how do you trace the effect of a change in some internal process on something like market position? The answer might be that if you can't identify a positive impact from the project on your corporate imperatives, why would you consider doing it?

Let me trace the path once more with an example. Assume you are considering benchmarking accounts receivable processes. Why do you want to do that? Obviously, you want to reduce your aging list and collect your money quickly so that your cash balance is as large as possible. But is that a major problem in your company? Money is important, but if you are awash in it while your customer relations are suffering, it makes sense to focus on customer relations. You might look first at your billing system. Are your invoices going out within twenty-four hours of shipment? Are they accurate? Are they readable? Are the terms clear? Is it your policy to have the salesperson follow up within a week to see if the customer has a problem with the invoice? Does the salesperson make sure that the product has been delivered as ordered? Paying attention to billing and shipping may do more for customer satisfaction than anything else you could do. The point is, your internal processes do affect customers. Put yourself in their shoes. What would you want? Are you giving the customers what they want? Are you better at it than your competition?

Now let's make it a little harder. Travel the better, faster, cheaper path. Assume that better billing is a possible benchmark project. What impact might improving facilities management have on your business? What is facilities responsible for? Do the facilities people get involved in office layout? What if they were to work with you to change the design of the accounting department so that there was a shorter physical distance between the accounting people who have to work together? Would this save time, improve relationships, build teamwork, and ultimately get those bills out the door faster, and cheaper? If the answer is yes, you now have a possible benchmarking project. How are the best accounting departments laid out? Benchmark that. Bring the data back for study. Did you learn anything that can be applied to your situation? If so, your project has added value.

It is possible that you would learn that physical layout is not the performance driver in the best-practice departments. They might rely on new electronic network technology. If that were your finding, you failed to confirm your original hypothesis but your project still succeeded. You learned what the critical variable is in best-practice accounts receivable departments.

Benchmarking is a collective learning experience. Its essence is that people learn from each other through benchmarking. Internally, you can learn from one another what makes you efficient and effective. You also develop a common vocabulary that will facilitate communication and understanding. You work together to solve problems rather than have an outsider do it for you. Externally, you learn together how you compare to other organizations and how you can be better. Because the process is participative, your people do the work, make the recommendations, and decide on when and how to make the changes. Even if you choose to employ a consultant, you still have the responsibility to see the project through.

4. Organizing and Training the Benchmarking Project Players

Who should be on the benchmarking team? Some people state that businesses should have benchmarking specialists who run projects for internal customers. I would be cautious here. If you build an internal capability, you are adding another function at the time most organizations are downsizing to control fixed costs. There are less costly ways to proceed. If you are in a start-up mode you will probably need some help with your first couple of projects. A number of qualified organizations exist that can help you. You can also join benchmarking networks. Many organizations are forming internal benchmarking groups. These are composed of people who have acquired the skills of benchmarking through outside training or experience. They can get you started. However, most benchmarking experts believe, as I do, that if benchmarking is going to become a value-adding tool, its skills will have to be acquired and used by all managers. Nothing endures unless it is part of the system. Eventually, you will want to make it your own.

If you say that you are already too busy to form your own benchmarking team, then you probably shouldn't consider benchmarking at all. If someone else does it for you, the process will involve you at both the front and back ends. To start with, an outsider will need time to become familiar with your operation. You will have to educate him. In the end he will know only what you tell him. When he goes to do the job for you he will be hampered by lack of in-depth knowledge. Unless he is extraordinarily insightful he will not have the background required to ask the second- and third-level questions. He won't notice the patterns that only an experienced professional would see. When he brings back the results, you will spend a lot more time with him debriefing to learn whether what he has learned is useful. You will ask those deeper questions and he won't have the answers. I can predict with utter certainty that you will be dissatisfied. Ultimately you must commit yourself to becoming involved.

Benchmarking Project Roles. There are several roles to be played in a staff benchmarking project: the process owner; the process stakeholders; the project leader; the project team, consisting of the data collectors and analysts; and the support staff. Their responsibilities are as follows:

•*Process owner.* This individual has control and authority over the process being studied. The process owner may or may not have commissioned the study. She is usually the manager of the unit wherein the process resides. She knows what the process is supposed to add to the business and may be aware of what needs to be done from a management perspective. Usually the process owner does not know the details of how the process is actually functioning or malfunctioning. However, she must be active in supporting the project, at least at a review level.

•*Process stakeholders.* These are people from other areas who are affected by the process. Since they are affected, they should be informed of what is contemplated and of how the study is progressing. They also have information on the inputs and outputs of the process and thus can be helpful in the diagnostic and final review stages.

•*Project leader.* This individual normally is an internal manager who may be supported by an outside benchmarking consultant. He directs the project by coordinating planning, staffing, directing, and scheduling, and by controlling the budget for the project. If the project is being done for an internal customer, the manager is the principal liaison between the customer and the project team. The project manager engages outside specialists, if needed, and monitors their performance against the project specifications. Where necessary, commitments for internal resources are obtained. The manager leads any group meetings and organizes any training that might be necessary.

•*Project team.* The team works on developing the instruments for data collection. Team members may contact benchmark partners and schedule data-collection calls or visits. They are often involved in collecting, summarizing, and analyzing the data. Under the guidance of the project manager, they identify performance gaps and often participate in presenting the report to management. The team is almost always composed largely of people from the process area. The full extent of their role is different in every organization. Cultural practices will determine who talks to whom and who will make presentations to management and stakeholders.

•*Support staff.* These workers are usually administrative personnel who might process data for analysts and produce the report documents. Support can include resources such as library services, transportation, data processing, or training. Legal counsel and other professional resources may be needed in some cases.

In order for all of the project members to play a useful part, they must be convinced in the beginning that this is a worthwhile use of their time. It is up to the project manager and any team members who are committed to the project to show others the value of this exercise. Assigning people to a project without gaining their commitment and providing them with whatever skills or resources they need to perform effectively can severely impede the undertaking.

Benchmarking is not mystical, but it is time-consuming. Still, it has the potential to be the most effective management tool you have ever used. The following is a short list of things you can do to get started.

Build Skills. The project manager needs experience in managing business units and must be able to work with top management. She should have knowledge of the process that will be benchmarked, and project management experience is a plus. Her most important abilities are oral and written communication skills.

The project team must contain all the skills and experience needed to carry out the work. These include detailed process knowledge and teamwork skills along with problem-solving, interviewing, analytic, and report writing/presenting capabilities. It is also very important that the team be committed to the project. Following is a guide for preparation:

1. *Read.* A few books and an increasing number of articles on benchmarking are available. Have your librarian research articles on the subject.

2. *Attend seminars.* The market for seminars on benchmarking is growing, with programs being offered by consulting companies and associations.

3. *Learn communications skills.* The most important skills for benchmarking are questioning and listening. Most of us have a lot to learn about how to be efficient communicators.

4. *Learn data skills.* Get the basics of data analysis from whatever source you can find. You must be able to understand what the data mean when you get them and then you must be able to interpret them.

Develop Relationships. The area in which an internal bench-marking project unit usually operates is in developing relationships. The staff have the time and charter to seek out resources to support internal projects. Listed are two places to begin:

1. *Join associations.* The American Productivity and Quality Center in Houston, Texas, is building a clearinghouse reference service for people who want to learn and practice benchmarking.

2. *Find networks.* Companies are banding together in benchmarking groups. The Saratoga Institute in Saratoga, California, and the Strategic Planning Institute in Cambridge, Massachusetts, have formed membership groups to support and conduct benchmarking projects. Others will follow.

Practice. One great advantage to having your people do their own benchmarking is that the project and its data are theirs. Following are possible starting points:

1. *Organize a small project.* Just do it. The risk is minimal and you have to start somewhere.

2. *Learn through experience.* Develop your expertise.

3. *Teach others.* Share your knowledge and skills with others in your unit and company. Eventually it will become part of the management system.

You have enlisted a work group whose members bring their individual skills, perceptive abilities, values, intuitions, and imaginations to the process. There is much less resistance to accepting the findings and trying to adapt some of them to your situation when your people have developed the data themselves. Along with that involvement comes the commitment to see the changes installed and maintained. The not-invented-here syndrome doesn't have a chance when your people do it themselves. Continuous improvement is based on involvement, without which the daily pressures and the power of tradition and habit will overwhelm your efforts.

5. Locating, Contacting, and Qualifying Benchmark Partners

The last planning step is sometimes the hardest. How do you know who is potentially a good partner? Unfortunately, there is no magic list of best-practice companies. You can never be absolutely certain you have identified the best. But you can still learn from anyone who is doing something well. Best-practice companies can be found among the following sources:

> *Publications:* articles, reports, and books
> *Experts:* experienced people from your industry or profession, and consultants
> *Meetings:* trade and professional shows and conferences
> *Associations:* trade and professional contacts and data bases
> *Personal contacts:* customers, suppliers, peers, board members

Each source offers a different set of potential partners. When you find several sources all pointing at one organization, there is a good chance you have found something. You won't really know until you talk with them, but at least you have narrowed the field. You may find the halo effect at work. Some companies such as Motorola, Xerox, Federal Express, 3M, and L.L. Bean have received a great deal of publicity in recent years. The fact that they are allegedly good at several functions does not necessarily mean that they are excellent at the function you want to benchmark. Reserve judgment until you have had a chance to talk with them.

Criteria for Selecting Benchmark Partners. When you look for benchmark partners for a large benchmarking project, scan the sources mentioned above with the following primary criteria in mind:

1. *Diversity.* Try to develop a cross section of different types of businesses, sizes of companies, and possibly geographic locations. It is useful to have companies from within your industry as well as from outside it. To a degree, the larger the field from which you choose, the better your chance of finding a world-class partner.

Each benchmark partner offers a different perspective on the topic. These diverse opinions and practices are the antecedents to insight. It is difficult to come up with a breakthrough when everyone is thinking the same way. Geography, competitive forces, growth rates, and size all stimulate different responses, each of which can be evaluated for its applicability to your situation.

2. *Creativity*. Is there innovation in what you hear or read about companies within the group? How far out are their ideas? Sometimes the wildest idea is the most useful. You can adapt an off-the-wall approach. If you don't want something different, you ought to stay home. Look for the kernel of value in the most creative and unique processes, policies, and practices. Don't let the craziness of an idea stop you from reviewing it. Just because you never would have considered it before doesn't mean it can't add value to your current situation.

3. *Desire*. Find people who are striving to be the best. This is sometimes a gut-reaction type of judgment. When you hear or read about their organization, what feeling do you get? Read between the lines. Is someone just exercising her ego in an article or a speech? Is the article a public relations job that the company probably paid for? Being the best is not an advertising project. Look for people who exude a desire to set the world on fire and to be the best.

The last two criteria may sound a little wild-eyed for serious business people, but one thing we need desperately in American companies today is a little more enthusiasm and leadership. Innovation and market creation never came from administrative thinking. I would rather have to throw cold water on someone than spend time trying to keep him awake.

Performance Drivers

Performance drivers are primary causal forces within an organization, which become the signature of the organization: The forces are a combination of environmental, structural, and activity factors. Collectively they describe why an organization's processes work the way they do. It is imperative that these drivers be identified if you wish to compare your organization to others. Figure 4.1 is a graphic example of what is included in performance drivers.

Figure 4.1. Typical Performance Drivers.

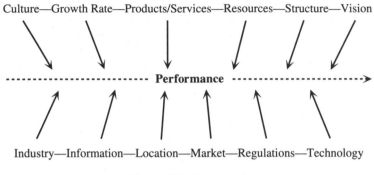

Internal Organizational

Culture—Growth Rate—Products/Services—Resources—Structure—Vision

Performance

Industry—Information—Location—Market—Regulations—Technology

External Environmental

Drivers can be internally or externally based. They can function at the strategic or tactical level. And they can be positive or negative. That is, they can support or inhibit the actions of a work group. Drivers that inhibit performance can be called constraints. Some drivers have been around since the founding of the company. Culture is an example. Stories of Thomas Watson setting the culture of IBM are legendary. The IBM culture served it well until recent years. Now, it is getting in the way of change. It is an example of a driver that has become a constraint. Other drivers have grown up with an industry. The electronics industry, which really emerged as a force about 1970, has always made relatively large investments in R&D compared to other industries. Until the mid 1980s it was also marked by heroic individualism and a distaste for governmental intervention. Other drivers are new, having resulted from a change in technology, the external market, or regulations. Worldwide recession, low consumer confidence, and tempered spending have become primary drivers for retailers. This in turn has caused them to cut back on advertising, thereby throwing a pall over the newspaper business. So, you can see how these types of forces can have a major effect on the way an organization operates from the strategic to the tactical levels.

The conditions described above clearly have an effect on every company. Both the best- and worst-practice companies are affected by their performance drivers. Many people have long claimed that their organization is unique and noncomparable. They are right in the first case and wrong in the second. Every organization is unique, but with care, organizations can be compared. What is needed to make judgments is a combination of insight, imagination, decisiveness, and a bit of risk taking. If you wait for a perfect match between companies, nothing will happen. Besides, it is not necessary.

Performance drivers can be applied either at the beginning of a project or later. When used as selection criteria, performance drivers are employed as follows:

1. Identify driving forces that might apply in this case.
2. Profile each potential partner's performance drivers.
3. Individually, look for similarities among the drivers.
4. Factor the difference and make your selections.

The second use of performance drivers comes later in the project. In steps one through four you gather driver data and file it in your mind. Then you proceed through the rest of the steps:

5. Collect the necessary benchmark data from your chosen partners.
6. Review the data, using the drivers as a filter.
7. Adapt what makes sense for you.
8. Take action.
9. Evaluate your results.
10. Repeat the cycle.

Remember that the objective is not perfection, it is progress. If you wait for perfection in business, you will soon be out of business.

Making Contact

What is the best way to know if you have the right partners? Talk to them. If they are close by, nothing is better than a visit.

Go to their site and meet them. Look around. Get a feel for the place. Is it humming? Is it the kind of environment that vibrates with improvement? A phone call may put you in touch with an enthusiast, but a visit will tell you whether something is really happening. Things are not always what they appear to be at first contact.

The Saratoga Institute was part of an international benchmarking project in early 1992. A group of Australians came to the United States to meet with some benchmarking partners that we had tentatively identified for them. After talking with one potential partner, they decided to visit his company. On their return they told us that the fellow had some good ideas that were useful. However, they doubted whether the ideas were being implemented. They told me they thought that if the zealot left the company nothing would change. He was making a lot of smoke but very little fire.

Having a clear idea of your own processes and what you want to know will help in selecting a partner. Incomplete preparation by your team can lead to a very diffused and unproductive effort. The Saratoga Institute managed a project for one company that could not get focused. Because it had started the project before we were called in, there was a great deal of personal ownership in it by that point. We tried to get people to focus and we had some degree of success, but not as much as we would have preferred. Rather than scrap what had already required months of effort by more than a dozen people, we decided to help them get something out of it. That was what we got — something. They had identified a couple dozen potential partners without doing much background research on any of them. It turned out that a number of the companies actually had very little to offer. The mass of data we collected for them was helpful, but it did not contain the specific magic answers they wanted. Better planning would have greatly reduced the amount of time and resources they spent and yielded vastly better results.

When you are preparing to make the contact, you should already have reviewed all relevant data available about the company. You know some of their performance drivers, but there are probably others that you didn't know about. For example, when you call the potential partner and find that the company is in the middle of a major downsizing, it is unlikely that they will want to engage in a project of any length with you. Assuming that you know all you can about the company, I suggest you follow a schedule something like this:

1. Call the company you think you want to benchmark with. Ask for the person who would know the most about the processes and metrics you have in mind.

2. Smile when she answers the phone. Your positive attitude will flow through to her.

3. Tell her who referred you or how you came to call her company.

4. Briefly describe your goal and ask if her company has an interest in discussing it.

5. Review the points and ask for the company's experience. Don't be a know-it-all; let her exercise her ego. You are calling to learn, not to preach. Check to learn if she has any hard data to support the claim that her company is getting better results than yours. This is where you will eliminate most of the useless contacts. The average — dare I call them mediocre — groups do not have good data available on their operation. That is one of the reasons they are average.

6. If you are satisfied, send the person a list of items you wish to discuss. This will give her a chance, off line, to think it over. If the company has little relevant data, she will probably tell you at that point. She will not want to waste her time any more than you will.

7. Offer an incentive for her company's participation: a copy of the project's findings, a complimentary tour of your facility, or something else that might tilt the decision in your favor.

8. Follow up and determine the company's decision. If they agree, ask if they have the time and resources to collect the data you will be benchmarking. Intent is good, commitment is imperative. If they agree, you have a partner. Now you can schedule the data-collection step.

Exhibit 4.3 provides an outline of the first part of a sample benchmarking project. It is structured around the five activities of the value-planning phase and is presented in sufficient detail to illustrate the real flavor of benchmarking.

Exhibit 4.3. Staff Benchmarking Project of the Sample Company:
Phase I. Value Planning.

1. *Identifying potential value opportunities*
   a. The accounting department was selected because the benchmarking team believed it offered high potential for adding value.
   b. The field was narrowed to the department where the best opportunity was thought to reside, taking into consideration people, processes, technology, and structure. The areas of potential improvement identified were:

   1. year-end tax preparation
   2. cost-accounting process
   3. accounts receivable process

2. *Assessing value potential*
   a. If the Sample Company were able to improve the three areas identified, where might the impact occur as in terms of the following: cost, time, quantity, quality, human reactions? That is, would the result be cheaper, faster, or increased production? higher quality? greater satisfaction? How would such improvements enhance Sample's competitive position?
   b. How much would the value added amount to annually measured in financial impact on each of the three areas? The preliminary estimates are as follows:

   1. About $50,000 saved in overtime, auditing, and possible penalties for late filing
   2. Potentially large effect on manufacturing, but unknown without major study
   3. At least $65,000 to $75,000 in faster receipt of payments, plus reductions in loan balances and probably improved relations with customers' accounts payable departments

3. *Selecting the benchmarking target*
   Based on the above estimates, Sample chose to start with the accounts receivable department while they undertook a study of the effects of the current cost accounting methods. What were the factors behind that decision? Further study revealed the following:

   Target: Accounts Receivable

   Reasons: Customers are paying in an average of seventy-five days. Industry average is fifty-two days. This is affecting cash flow and bank balances. We believe part of the problem is our invoicing process and our forms, which some customers claim are confusing and often have errors in them. The confusing process/forms not only slow down payment but also adversely affect customer relations. In addition, since many of our customers are located on the West Coast, we lose a few days in mailing. Also, when the collections department calls them, customers claim they never received our invoices.

**Exhibit 4.3. Staff Benchmarking Project of the Sample Company:
Phase I. Value Planning, Cont'd.**

---

4. *Forming the benchmarking team*
   a. Who should be on the team?

Project leader	Senior Accountant Smith
Accounting Director	Senior Accountant Jones
Manager, Accounts Receivable (A/R)	Several other accounting personnel

   Chief Finance Officer (CFO) and Controller will be on review team along with Sales Manager, who is concerned about customer relations.
   b. Are any skills needed?
   Yes, manager, A/R, and senior accountants will be calling and perhaps visiting benchmarking partners. They need training in interviewing and data analysis.
   c. Schedule the training.

5. *Locating and contacting benchmarking partners*
   a. Where will Sample's benchmarking team look for partners?
      1. Publications: on-line data-base search for success story articles? Yes.
      2. Experts? No.
      3. Meetings: upcoming regional accounting conference? Yes.
      4. Professional association? No.
      5. Personal contacts? Will call selected professional acquaintances.
   b. Contact: Who will make qualifying contacts with the potential benchmarking partners and how?
      1. Project leader will direct data-base search by library.
      2. Senior accountant Smith will attend regional conference.
      3. A/R manager, Smith, and Jones will call professional peers.

Value-Planning Phase Progress Report: Five partner companies have agreed to participate. The training has been taken and the Sample team is ready to begin the Data Development phase.

Conclusion

Few benchmarking projects finish with a product that is better than the planning was. You have to know what values you seek. You have to be able to tell yourself and anyone who asks what "better" would look like. And you should be able to project a dollar-target goal of improvement before you start. This is not an exercise in financial projection, but you need a target to keep you on track.

Lay Out a Structure

What is the target function? What is the process area? Which activities will you focus on? What outcomes do you expect to achieve? There is an endless supply of benchmark opportunities. Finding the place with the greatest return on your investment is not always easy. Look for linkage from internal processes to external effects. Discuss the linkages between process, outcome, impact, and value added. Consider the positions of the key support players: top management, major stakeholders. What does all this tell you? Decide which is the best opportunity and which can be achieved. Sometimes the greatest gains are not possible at this point. You may have to work up to the blockbuster. Pick the low-hanging fruit first.

Recruit the Benchmarking Team

These are the people who will make the difference. Involving them, giving them real power to act and add value, will pay off with a better process and more useful results. Prepare them with the training and resources they will need. Success requires investment. Quick and dirty just makes a mess. If you can't invest in a big project right now, start with a small one. Gain commitment from the team members to devote their hearts and hands to this project. Organize them and lay out a schedule.

Search Out Benchmarking Partners

The number of sources is growing, but you have to find them. Read, attend conferences, talk to people. Look for diversity, creativity, and desire within your potential partners. Dig out their performance drivers. Beware of the halo effect. Our experience is that few, if any, organizations are excellent throughout. Many are very strong in certain areas and relatively weak in others. Your learning will only be as good as the benchmark partners you select.

5

Data Development:
Gathering Useful Information

Data management is paradoxically the most interest-
ing as well as one of the most difficult and occasion-
ally tedious aspects of benchmarking. Many staff profes-
sionals and managers worldwide are not highly skilled
in quantitative and qualitative data analysis. There
is both art and science to data gathering and interpre-
tation. Successful benchmarking demands data systems
and skills.

This is where the fun begins. It is what you have
been waiting for. The best part of benchmarking is meeting and
talking with your benchmarking partners. If you have done a
good job of planning the project, selecting and preparing your
team, and initiating contact with your partner, this phase will
be a fruitful experience. If you have not planned carefully and
completely, however, you run the risk of producing a product
of limited value. This chapter deals with what you do to develop the data you need and want in the most efficient and enoy-
able manner.

Assume that you have contacted and qualified your partner or partners. They know what you want and they are prepared to share data with you on certain processes or practices.
Now, you move to data development. There are several steps
to this phase:

1. Develop a questionnaire.
2. Select a method of data collection and schedule the contact with your benchmarking partner.
3. Send the project portfolio to your partner and carry out the data collection.
4. Organize and analyze the data.

The first two items are interdependent. As you are developing your questions you will begin to think about the best way to present them — through telephone interviews, surveys, focus groups, or a combination of these and other methods that will be described in this chapter.

Start at Home

In order to make sense of your partners' data you need to know how your company is doing on the function you are benchmarking. After all, this is an exercise in comparative analysis. You have to ask and answer every question about your own process before you approach other people about theirs. You need to know in detail where you stand so that you can make meaningful comparisons. This can be done at two levels. If the topic is relatively straightforward and if there is no other group within your own company with which you might benchmark, you can proceed to document and measure your process in preparation for an external project. First, however, it may be worthwhile to run an internal minibenchmark project with another internal function's process. Again, you start by documenting your own process and then examine your benchmarking partner. This practice gives you some experience. Your team will develop benchmarking skills that will make them more efficient and credible when you initiate an external project.

Another reason for internal benchmarking is that you may be able to solve your problem or exploit your opportunity without having to carry out a lengthy external benchmarking project. At least it gives you a first benchmark. Now you have some sense of where you stand. Later on if you do go outside, you and your people will be able to talk with greater facility and knowledge about the process. You will know your process better because you will have already explained it to someone inside your own organization. Your external benchmarking partner will feel confident that he or she is dealing with well-prepared, knowledgeable people.

Questionnaire Design

Designing a questionnaire is a multistep process. Decisions must be made about the form, number, and content of questions. They have to be organized logically, and the instrument must be tested to be sure it is understandable.

Structure of Questions

Choose the question structure most appropriate to the issue under investigation. There are several general types of questions. Exhibit 5.1 provides examples of each type. You should select the ones you use based on how much detail you need and whether you want the respondent to make a statement or some type of comparison. I find that open-ended questions yield better results when they are presented as requests for descriptions. The responses seem to be more detailed and usually produce more amplifying information. I believe people give information requests more thought when they are asked for a description, although I can't prove it. Both open-ended and descriptive responses often reveal why there are differences between the various benchmarking partners. As such, they are very useful methods of inquiry.

The different types of questions can be intermixed as long as the questionnaire does not become confusing. On the other hand, if you ask a long series of scaled questions you risk what is called *response set*. In this phenomenon the respondent gets locked into a mental position and tends to score many of the questions at the same point on the scale. For this and other reasons it is useful to have a professional help you develop your questionnaire if it will run more than a page or two. A few dollars spent here can save a great deal of time trying to sort out confusing responses or struggling with data that are clearly suspect.

Exhibit 5.1. Types of Question Structure.

Multiple choice: What drove your decision to design the process as it is?

_____ cost

_____ cycle time

_____ volume of work anticipated

_____ level of quality required

_____ reduction in worker stress

Forced choice: Do you consider cost or quality to be more important?

_____ cost

_____ quality

Comparative: Do you consider quality to be the most important issue?

_____ Yes

_____ No

Scaled: How much effect does your strategic plan have on operating decisions?

| A great deal | Some | Not much | It is ignored |

Open-ended: How do you qualify your office supply vendors?

Descriptive: Please describe how you qualify your office supply vendors.

Number of Questions

How many questions should you ask? How long should the questionnaire be? I have heard benchmarking "experts" suggest that you shouldn't ask more than a half dozen questions. I have also heard them say that you can have fifteen pages of questions. Who is right? The answer is found in the problem. How large a process or how many processes are you taking on? I've seen questionnaires more than twenty pages long because that many questions were required to cover the scope of the processes being benchmarked. Frankly, that is too long. The data-handling job alone is so cumbersome that the results are delayed and insights are hard to come by. In addition, very few people can stand to plow through that much information when it is presented to them. There is no magic answer regarding the number of questions that can or should be asked. Just keep two things in mind: start small, because the scope of the project and the questionnaire will grow; be reasonable. Don't try to solve the mystery of life.

Content of Questions

I suggest that you involve the people who are working the process in preparing questions. For example, if you are going to study accounts receivable you will want some of the accountants from your accounts receivable department on the team. They know the processes and can help form appropriate questions. They probably already have some questions such as, "Why do we take Step X? It doesn't seem to add anything and just delays the process." Questions like this may even bring out the insights you need to improve the process without having to benchmark it.

As a consultant I frequently find myself in situations where initially I know very little about the problem at hand. I usually start by asking the purpose and objectives of the issue—in this case, the process. Let me give you an example.

On one occasion I was called in to design a method for evaluating a specialized planning process. Frankly, I didn't know whether it could be done. However, never letting ignorance stand in my way, I jumped in. There were just four basic issues to clarify:

1. What exactly were they doing in the process? I asked them to list the steps that I could see them doing.

2. Why were they doing each step? What was the purpose or objective? The answers had to be expressed as some visible objective or outcome.

3. What effects did they expect those outcomes to achieve in the organization? Of course, the effects had to be stated as something visible, such as a reduction in a cost, in turnover, or in process time.

4. The last question was obvious: How would they measure those outcomes? What ratios could they apply that could be converted to quantitative value?

The point is that if you start by asking what is being done and why, you can usually trace the process through a series of visible steps to a measurable outcome.

After clarifying the strategic-level issues of purpose and objectives, I often follow the reporter's path of asking who, what, where, when, why, how, and how much—although not necessarily in that order. For example:

> What is the process? (short descriptive title)
>
> How does the process work? (flow chart)
>
> Who is involved in the process? (all the players active in and related to the process even if only in a reporting role)
>
> Why are they involved? (What is their role and why aren't certain other people included?)
>
> Where does each player reside in the flow? (sequential position)
>
> When do certain things happen? (includes how often)
>
> How much does it cost? (people, time, commitment of material resources)

You can then begin to probe for problems: What is wrong? Why is it wrong? Who is involved in the problem?

Asking the right question is obviously the key to obtaining the most useful answer. You should ask for the data elements—How many people do you have in your department?" or "How many people are employed in your company?"—as well as for the ratios you really want to know—"What is the ratio of people in your department to people served in the company?" By having both raw numbers and ratios you can cross-check. Staff people are often quite imprecise in reporting quantitative data. Each year, when we compile our national human resource effectiveness report, we cross-check every one of the more than twenty-five thousand figures submitted. The incidence of error is such that we take nothing for granted.

Questionnaire Organization and Layout

The next step in questionnaire design is to organize the questions. Begin at the beginning. Again, what is the purpose of this project? What do we need to know to identify gaps and make improvements that will ultimately yield the added value we predicted? Each question asked should be absolutely necessary. Start with the most general and move to the more specific. Will you need both current and past data to uncover trends and project the future? A very useful technique is to diagram your questions as you think of them — that is, arrange them by category. This will illustrate where you are drifting off the key points. Some natural drift will occur when you talk to your partners later. So, keep the original list as focused as possible.

Balance the questionnaire. Give each topic an appropriate number of questions. Don't overkill. There seems to be a tendency, particularly when a team is designing a questionnaire, to ask more questions than you need. The unspoken idea seems to be that if two questions are good, four will be better. Ask yourself, if I had the answer to this question what could I do with it? Develop a logic and flow to the list of questions. Start with the most general and move to the more specific.

Be sure to avoid leading questions. Whether you will be asking your questions face-to-face or using a document structure, prepare unbiased questions so that you don't prejudice the response. A simple example is to ask, "What types of computers do you think are the most cost effective in this process?" rather than, "Don't you think that minicomputers are the most cost effective solution here?" Often people will not agree with your opinion based on good data from their experience. Yet, rather than disagree with you and risk a long debate or argument, they will go along — you'll have missed a chance to learn something of value.

Last, but very important, a set of questions covering issues of comparability needs to be asked in the beginning. Demographic information on the internal organizational drivers/constraints described in Chapter Four should be requested at the start. You want to determine early whether anything inside the potential benchmark company makes it noncomparable with your firm. Next should come questions regarding external drivers/constraints. Market, technology, and other issues should be explored here. The reason for putting comparability questions at the top of the form is obvious. You don't want to enter several pages of data only to find at the end that you can't use them.

The longer your questionnaire, the more critical is its format or layout. Designing a format that will lead the reader easily through the list of questions is not difficult. However, if your questions have subdivisions or any other twists and turns, your design can be important.

For printing the questionnaire, I favor large-size typeface, at least 12 point, for easier reading. Use a serif typeface, one with the little hooks and lines on the letters, like the type in this book. Studies have shown that serif faces are easier to read than sans serif faces. Since you will probably be working with a computer word processing program, it will be easy to use boldface, italics, or different typefaces to highlight different aspects. But don't get too fancy. Too many variations can confuse, fatigue, and distract the reader. It is better to apply format options judiciously to direct the readers without dazzling them with your computer virtuosity.

Testing the Questionnaire for Clarity

Make sure the questions are easy to understand. Many benchmarking projects have failed at the first step because of unclear questions. Test the questions on someone. Before you mail the questionnaire or give it to telephone interviewers, read the questions to someone to learn whether they are understandable. Next, send the questionnaire out to be tested when you aren't around to provide any prompts. Ask your readers to make notes for you regarding any problems and also to put down how long it took to answer the questions. Finally, ask them which questions would have required them to go into the records to gather data that were not readily available.

You will find that it is often necessary to provide definitions of terms. Even the most common terms, such as revenue and operating expense, are calculated differently in various industries. The most prominent examples are the banking and insurance industries, which define revenue differently from the manufacturing industry. A glossary of terms is useful if you have a long questionnaire.

Remember that you also have to answer these questions

about your own organization. Since benchmarking is data sharing, you will need to have your data ready before you talk to your partners. You may experience difficulties when attempting to answer your own questions. If backup data are needed, they might not be readily obtainable, or you may not be able to share them. Later, when you have found the answers and the backup data, it could be helpful to tell your partners how you did it. We often see potential survey or benchmarking partners turn down a project because they do not know how to acquire some necessary data. Being able to tell them how to uncover it can win over a participant to your project.

Avoid in-house jargon. Make believe that someone who has a very limited knowledge of your benchmarking process and has never had contact with your organization must understand and transmit the questions to someone who will eventually develop the data. This happens. It is also a good idea to use as little professional jargon as possible. You might be surprised at the subtle differences that are applied to professional shorthand in different organizations. Having to redo the questionnaire in midstream or recheck all the data when you discover that different people thought you meant different things can be a real nuisance.

At Typically Ltd., the benchmarking participants eventually will spend a lot of time interacting across departments. This will also be true as they gather data with their benchmarking partners. They will have to ask the partners how their staff departments' processes and outputs affect each other and affect the line functions. It will happen again when they analyze their findings and prepare an action plan. In a complex case like this, it is a good idea to follow the basic KISS principle: Keep It Simple, Sherlock.

An Application

The following example shows how questions might be developed and arranged in solving a real problem: The real estate lease management department of a major chemical company decided it needed to make improvements in its leasing processes.

The department members started by identifying their basic business purpose and then searching for the best topic to benchmark. The topic was chosen based on its having the highest value potential for the department's customers, the managers of the company. Department members asked themselves what the customers valued in a space-leasing service and how the customers measured lease-management performance. Then, they developed several metrics to show themselves how good they were in these areas.

The next step was to create a flow chart of the leasing process. After that they found benchmarking partners and developed a questionnaire covering the steps in the process. The following questions address the first two steps. (Notice how the questions follow the reporter's method described earlier.)

Step 1. Request for Space.

How are requests received?
Who makes requests?
Who receives requests?
How much lead time is there usually and how is this time managed?
What alternatives do requesters have for fulfilling their needs?
How often do they choose an alternative?
Why do they choose an alternative?
How do requesters know about your service?
What percentage of the space your company leases is handled by your department?

Step 2. Needs Analysis.

Describe the process you use for needs analysis.
How involved is the person requesting space?
How much time is usually committed to the needs analysis?
Is the analysis reviewed with the space requester? How often?
Do you have standards for space utilization? Are they corporate or regional?

How are standards brought into the needs-analysis process?
What authorization is required to exceed standards?
Who can authorize?
What percentage of the time are the standards exceeded?

These questions were typed up and sent to the benchmarking partners after an initial phone conversation. The questions for each step were written in sequence as a single paragraph. This made the response requirement appear less formidable.

Selecting a Data-Collection Method

The questionnaire can be employed in several ways to collect the benchmark data — surveys, telephone interviews, site visits, and others. Choosing the one or two methods that are most appropriate for you depends on several considerations. You will find that the methods and questions overlap. Picking the right combination will enrich your results. The issues to keep in mind as you are deciding on which methods to employ are discussed below.

- *Time, budget, and staff resources available.* How much time do you expect this project will take in terms of total team-member hours? What will it cost in terms of hours, materials, computer time, travel if that might be necessary, consultants if you need them, and so on? Whatever it is, double it. As someone once said, everything takes twice as long as you expect and costs twice as much as you budgeted.
- *Uses for the data.* Who is going to use the data and what will they be doing with them? Resolving this issue will help you answer most of the following questions. Give this sufficient thought before making plans for data collection. It is generally a sound principle to involve the users somehow in the project so that they take ownership of the data. Excluding them enhances the possibility that they will reject the findings. In such a case, the whole project is worse than a waste of time. This outcome frustrates the project team and turns people off the whole idea of benchmarking. It leads to the not-invented-here excuse.

- *Type of data needed.* How complex is the information you need to gather? How many sources will you have to tap? How deep will you have to dig? Do you need historic data or trends? Benchmarking projects tend to multiply like rabbits once you set them free. You start down a central path and come across some interesting related information. It is a great temptation to follow it, so build in a little wandering time. Again, whatever you project, double it just to be safe.
- *Location of the data.* Will you have to travel? Will data-base searches be necessary? This will probably be the easiest question to answer.
- *Amount of data required.* How much information do you need as a bare minimum to fulfill your primary mission? Can you answer your questions by talking to one partner or will you need to obtain data from several?
- *Level of detail required.* Are you looking for basic trends or do you need specific, task-level details? Can you achieve sufficient depth of detail through oral discussion or will you have to study records as well? Will you need to run various statistical operations? Who will do that for you?
- *Quality of data desired.* How important is the level of accuracy? Deciding this will help you answer the previous question. If you have to reach a certain level of profound detail, does that imply the need for statistics? This is seldom the case in staff benchmarking. I often find that the only people who insist on statistical validity are corporate research staffs who don't have any real idea of what is going on in your function.
- *Skills in data collection.* Are special skills required? Does your team currently have those skills? If not, where can they be acquired? How long will it take to do that? This is where you may have to revise the kickoff date of the project or reestimate the total time of the project because critical skills may not be readily available. To launch a program with people who are essentially incompetent in interviewing skills is a waste of time. I have seen major disappointments result from an underestimation of the skills demanded.
- *Organizational norms for data collection and sharing.* I have talked about the effect of culture on organizational work. When we try to do something in a way that does not conform to the

norms of our organization, we are doomed. At best, we put in a great deal of effort to achieve sub-optimal results. The experience is like swimming into a strong current. What types of organizational issues will affect the way you go about collecting data inside and outside the organization? What is the cultural norm about sharing data? What can be shared and what can't?

There is no standard for selecting which methods to employ. I can tell you what others have done, but that has little bearing on what you should do. Stick with the principles I am outlining and you will do fine. Review the list. Answer each of the choices. Then, make a decision on what is best for you. The task of reviewing the list will help you realize what you are involved in. As you review each method, you will begin to sense what is required. For example, how much time, money, or people do you have to devote to benchmarking this process? If the answer is not much of any of them, then you obviously have to pick the fastest, cheapest method and accept what that is likely to yield. However, what most often happens is conflict. You need a lot of data with some level of detail and absolute quality, yet you don't feel you have the resources to commit right now. It's decision time. What are the trade-offs? Can you accept a lower level of output at this time? Perhaps you can cut back on the scope and still develop something of value within the resource commitment that you can make. Benchmarking is like many tasks. Often you don't have optimum conditions, but you do the best you can and go on. It's usually better to do a little bit well rather than to do a lot poorly.

There are advantages and disadvantages to each method of data collection, of which there are two general types: data research and personal contact. The methods along with their good points and drawbacks are described below.

Research

The research method is subdivided into three types: publications, electronic data bases, and reverse engineering. Although thousands of articles from the many trade and professional publications are on electronic data bases, you can also find casual pieces that can be useful in newspapers and other general interest sources. They can lead you toward potential benchmark partners. Reading product literature and public information is part of research. An in-house library staffed by professional librarians can be very helpful. These people live to do research. Checking out publications and stocking shelves does not thrill them. They love to dig for data; the more obscure, the better. It is their raison d'être. I have always found librarians to be extremely cooperative. If you don't have a corporate library you can get help from the public library. The research departments in large libraries usually will look up items for you provided you don't make a pest of yourself. They also have on-line data bases that you can access by yourself.

Document research must be organized. Since such a wealth of data is available these days, it is easy to bury yourself in it. I suggest you create a filing system for data you collect. Where possible, group related data so that a review of a file will begin to yield correlations. A little organization on the front end will save hours of confusion and possibly missed information later on.

The obverse of organizing is reverse engineering, a process of getting your hands on something and disassembling it. By taking something apart you see what goes into it, how it was made, and how it is capable of doing what it does. This is a favorite technique of engineers. The Japanese did it to American products with great success. Engineers all over the world do it. When the first portable computers came out in the late 1970s, every computer manufacturer begged, bought, or in some cases actually stole one and took it apart to learn how the miniaturization was accomplished.

You can reverse-engineer a process or an entire function if you have detailed information on all the steps. Assembly lines, administrative work-flow diagrams, and any other process or department that can be accurately and completely represented on paper, film, videotape, or a computer screen can be reverse-engineered. What you have to figure out is the thought process that went into the design. Why does the flow go this way and why are there approvals, copies distributed, or other side steps taken at certain points? To benchmark the process you also have to know the specifications. What is the cost to run it? What is the cycle time? What is the output-to-input ratio? What is the error or defect rate? What effect does it have on the people running it? If you know the answers to those questions you can then compare that process to your process.

Personal Contact

There are several types of personal contact methods. Probably the most commonly used are telephone interviews and surveys. Another method of personal contact is the focus group. It can be used when the people involved are in the same geographic area. Personal site visits are very popular but not always possible because of distance and budget problems. If the project goes beyond the local area, travel can be expensive and time-consuming. This is a particularly sensitive issue when budgets are tight or performance requirements are escalating. These four methods of personal contact are discussed below.

Telephones. Telephone interviews offer the best combination of speed, cost, and detail. With this method, you can talk with a large number of benchmarking partners in a relatively short time. Also, a lot of data can be obtained through a well-designed and well-conducted telephone interview. It gives you the chance to go into detail and ask second- and third-level questions. You can also repeat questions and ask for clarification if you don't understand the response. Finally, you can recap key points to verify what you have heard. But telephone interviewing does require some skill. The most important steps are preparation and focus. This is not to be a casual conversation. The interviewee's time must be respected.

Since telephones are everywhere, especially with the proliferation of portables and car phones, you have plenty of opportunity to make contact. Telephoning is the most flexible method. You can call from home, office, airport, airplane, automobile, or any other place that has a public phone or where you can use your portable. On the other hand, telephones have some inherent problems. The person you want is not always available, especially if he or she is not anticipating your call. A game of telephone tag can be time-consuming and frustrating. Some people don't like long phone conversations and may restrict your calling to clarifying previously submitted written data. As a general rule, it is a good idea—as well as considerate—to submit questions in writing to the other person before you call. This preview allows him or her time to give some thought to your data needs and to do whatever research is needed to prepare for your call. This preparation is very desirable because spur-of-the-moment responses usually produce incomplete and sometimes inaccurate data.

Surveys. A survey is an economical way to collect a large amount of data from a large population. Although it can be very cost efficient, to be effective the survey document must be well constructed. There is a science to designing an effective questionnaire to collect a large amount of information. What you ask, how you ask it, the sequence of topics, and the format are all important. If you have only a half dozen questions with no secondary level of detail involved you can simply list the queries in a logical descending order of general to specific. But when you want to know many things about many topics, then the design becomes important. Design is also important for data transfer. If you have several benchmarking partners submitting data you will need to record, calculate, and summarize it in ways that make it easily readable and comparable.

The downside with surveys is that the return rate is generally quite low. In general surveying, 15 percent to 20 percent return is considered good. Benchmarking surveys do better because the survey recipients usually have been forewarned and have agreed to participate. Surveys also are inflexible. You get answers only to what you have asked. There is no chance to ask second- or third-level questions. You also don't have a sense of how confident the respondents are in their data. On the phone you can hear how they sound. If they are guessing, their uncertainty usually comes through.

Surveys are often used in connection with telephone interviews. This was the method used in the case I will describe in Chapter Nine. After qualifying the partners by phone, each was sent a survey document by mail. The survey was then followed by a telephone discussion. We did not go over the points one by one because the questionnaire was too long. We did try to fill gaps between the questions, clarify any questions that were unclear, and validate the information we had received.

Focus Groups. Focus groups offer you the advantage of obtaining the opinions and knowledge of a number of interviewees at one time. This is a technique used by market researchers. By putting a group together and structuring their discussion, you can learn a great deal more than you can from spending the same number of hours with one person at a time. Focus groups function well when the topic is relatively straightforward. They also work well when group members have similar needs and common experience and skill levels. By carefully selecting homogeneous groups you can learn the opinions, needs, and fears of population segments. Heterogeneous groups tend to generate "average" information. For example, if you wanted to know the human-factor issues involved in a certain operation, it would be best to separate the operators from the designers and the managers. The experience, vested interests, and therefore viewpoints of these groups are obviously quite different.

The focus group method works better on some processes than on others. The more complex the issue, the more difficult it is to use a focus group. Lots of time is consumed in clarifying terms and debating subtle but often meaningless points. In addition, some people don't function well in groups. The more complicated the topic, the more their dysfunctional traits emerge and affect everyone in the group. It takes a skilled facilitator to bring out everyone's views, keep the dominant types from running over the submissives, and move the discussion along at just the right pace.

Site Visits. Personal meetings at the partner's site are the best method of data collection from a quality and quantity standpoint. You have a chance to build a personal relationship, which tends to open up the discussion. You and your partner connect and, if all goes well, build trust. Because you have traveled to the site, your partner is likely to spend a good deal of time with you. A site visit also gives the other company time to explore their interests more thoroughly. In the long term you will have established a friendly, professional relationship that can be helpful on other matters as well. Always remember what your mother taught you about good manners. Keep in mind that you are visiting someone's home. Respect his or her time and customs. Be prepared, be focused, don't probe issues your partner is apparently reluctant to discuss. It's better to leave a little short on data and keep a friend.

It is all right to take notes during your visit. You can't be expected to remember everything. But it is also a good idea to ask first if your partner minds your taking notes. Also, ask him or her to tell you when it isn't okay. It may be that someone doesn't want their floor layout diagrammed. You should know that so no one is embarrassed later. Keep your antennae up. Open your eyes and ears. When you have finished your visit, offer your benchmarking partner a visit to your site. It is common courtesy and gives you another chance to develop more data.

The chief drawbacks of site visits are the time and expense incurred. This is where the trade-off comes. Do you make contact from a distance and save money or do you risk the expense of travel in the hopes of greatly increasing the data you receive? The answer goes back to the beginning of the process: your choice is a matter of perceived value. What is it worth to you to get what you need? How will it affect your operation? You may want to restrict your site visits to those that offer the greatest perceived value. If you have done a good job of value planning, you should have an idea of what the payoff will be. You can save travel money by combining your benchmarking visit with another business trip. As an alternative, you can agree to meet your partner at a conference or convention that you both plan to attend. The tradeoff for convenience in that case will be that you won't be able to see your partner's process in operation. Seeing is worth more than a survey or telephone call.

It is almost certain that you will employ a combination of the various methods outlined above. Most likely you will gather some data from researching data bases and other public information sources. This will lead to your identifying a list of potential partners whom you will call. From there you might decide to gather the next round of data by using a survey form. This is an inexpensive alternative. Then, if it is warranted, you might agree to site visits to finish off the fine points.

In our process we always suggest a round table as the final step. Here the participants come together for a day or two to review the results. This review is just another form of data collection. It is an opportunity to dig out the most subtle nuances of the findings and to gain deeper insights.

The Project Portfolio

Nothing beats preparation. In this case I am talking about preparing your partners, helping them to do a good job. Before you contact your benchmark partners to do your data gathering, send them a project portfolio. This packet contains all the data they need to prepare themselves. It includes the following:

1. *The project purpose.* Outline why you are doing the project, the areas you will be exploring with your partners, and why they have been asked to participate, listing their particular strengths.
2. *Your team members.* Include a brief introductory sheet on each team member working on the project. Even if you don't anticipate direct contact between the partner and most of the team, it is good to list all team members. Including them all is an act of courtesy, and it is possible that the partner may call one of them later.
3. *Benchmark partners.* Make a list, complete with phone, fax, and mail data, that includes all the partners. It is only fair that everyone on your team should know who is in the game. Later, there may be reason for them to contact each other. Don't forget to include contact information on yourself.

4. *Project schedule.* Outline key information in a project sched-
    ule. Include the time and date of each event as presently
    scheduled. Also list the contact people and those who will
    facilitate any group meetings. If the partner is to provide
    any materials or facilities, that should be noted.
5. *Topic specifics.* Going beyond the simple listing of the func-
    tions that will be explored, next provide either an outline
    of the processes to be investigated or in some cases the spe-
    cific questions that will be discussed. Issues of proprietary
    information should be noted. This is also a good place to
    state your organization's ethics policy.
6. *Cover letter.* Tell your partner you appreciate his or her
    cooperation. A cover note thanking the person for agree-
    ing to help satisfy your needs is always appropriate.

Ethical Issues

I don't need to tell you not to ask for proprietary information.
It is a good practice to discuss rules related to proprietary information at the outset. Be clear with all parties about what is
off-limits. If proprietary information does come up and you want
to discuss it, you should get prior permission from all concerned.

   If there are copyright or patent issues, you may need permission from the patent or legal department. The partners
should prepare a written request for permission stating the reasons such information is needed. This would be followed by a
written agreement, a nondisclosure agreement, signed by both
parties and decribing the limits of approved use.

   Several specific practices should be considered unethical
when you are gathering data. Most of them involve common
sense. The following are the primary ethical issues:

1. Benchmarking is not an excuse for recruiting. The contacts
    made and the visits to plant sites should never be under-
    taken with the idea of uncovering candidates for a job in
    your company. This is especially important if the hire is
    a hidden attempt to obtain competitive information.
2. Never misrepresent yourself or your purpose. Play the game

properly and expect others to do the same. Let your partners know in the beginning the true and full scope of your interests.

3.   Do not take photographs unless doing so is explicitly approved ahead of time.

4.   Do not share benchmarking information with third parties without express permission from your benchmarking partners.

5.   Do not ask for cost or pricing information unless that is an explicit part of the project. As a general rule, any financial data that are not available through public sources should not be sought or discussed.

6.   Share your organization's ethics policy with your benchmarking partners at the front end of the project if you might be dealing in sensitive areas later.

The best practice is, as always, the golden rule.

Data Preparation and Analysis

Data analysis starts with data organization. You can't analyze something you can't comprehend. If several people are working in tandem, it is very useful to get them together shortly after collecting data on each phase to review the information you have at that time. The longer you wait, the more likely you are to miss the fine points. Here is a simple procedure:

- Organize the data section by section. It is extremely helpful to record the information on flip charts that everyone can see.
- Have each person in turn identify the key points obtained and any implications they suggest. Do this until all have described their work in that section.
- Consolidate the data on the flip charts into a final set of observations on that section. Then, move the group to the next section and repeat the process.
- When all sections have been covered, compile the data in an electronic file and distribute an interim report to all team members.

Neatly cataloguing or arranging the data in an electronic file will save you lots of time when you need to search for something later. Having organized your information, you are ready to analyze it.

The next step is to review the data for three attributes: relevance, completeness, and accuracy. Did you get what you went after? Has anything happened since you started the project that has changed or expanded its focus? Often you will find that the study expanded beyond its original parameters. There is nothing wrong with that so long as you are collecting information that will be useful. The second question is, did you get everything you need? Sometimes you will find that you need to go back and pick up some point of information that was missed. This can happen if the interview got off track at some point. I find that when you are benchmarking with several partners it is easy to miss something with one of them. It may be that you obtained enough from the others and that they all tended to agree on the point. In that case there is no need to go back to the one that you missed. The last area is accuracy. Are the data valid? Did the respondents interpret your questions properly and answer correctly? If there are errors, they could have occurred in recording and transferring the responses. I once flipped a scale, recording the "strongly *dis*agree" responses as "strongly agree" responses. As a consequence, the preliminary report suggested a surprising result. On reexamination of the scale, my error became apparent. I don't have to tell you I was embarrassed.

The third step is to shape the data and calculate any statistics required. If you are convinced the data are accurate, you can begin to format them. If you are working with several companies, it is helpful to construct matrices for the quantitative data. List the companies on one axis and the data categories on the other. This graphic gives you a quick view of all data on a comparative basis. Anomalies pop out and say, "Look at me." You will also see patterns when you juxtapose related data. In a study done by the Saratoga Institute of the hiring processes of six insurance companies, we stacked data on total employees, number of hires, and turnover rates. Immediately it became clear that something was wrong. Total staff was unchanged, yet hiring was high and turnover was low. It didn't make sense. If we had looked only horizontally across the spreadsheet, we would not have noticed that some of the data were inaccurate.

In dealing with quantitative data it is wise to stick with simple arithmetic calculations. Highs, lows, and means usually do the trick. Only if you have many companies participating might you want to calculate a standard deviation. Usually you are working with just a few companies, so the distribution of data points is not meaningful. Sophisticated statistical procedures are seldom necessary. Of course, there are always exceptions to any generalization. In complex matters, statistics are useful, but these cases are very rare, especially in staff functions. Besides, most people don't remember the statistics they learned in college and others avoided the subject altogether. I can't think of any situation in my fifteen years of measuring the effectiveness of staff functions in which complex statistics would have added significant, practical value. The fact is simply that if you can't see the obvious value differences using means, modes, medians, and standard deviations, multiple regressions seldom are illuminating.

Next, prepare whatever graphs might be useful. These help the project team see the differences. They also help later on when you are preparing a report for someone outside the team. If you have a large number of participants, a scattergram is useful to show how each partner compares individually with every other partner. Depending on your rules of disclosure you might not identify each company in the chart.

Finally, summarize the commentary data. Verbatim regurgitations usually are not in order. However, there are exceptions to that rule. A review of the verbal responses to each question will tell you which way to lay out the narrative. The main requirement is to synthesize the key points so that all participants can draw their own conclusions. Remember, there is no one right answer. The data will suggest different things to each company. When each partner takes into consideration his or her firm's performance drivers, each will have to decide what the data mean in that particular case.

Be careful not to overwork the information. This investigation is not doctoral dissertation research. You need only a degree of precision sufficient to make decisions. Two or three decimal points is usually more than enough for investigating any administrative process. The key is not to get tied up in data analysis. It doesn't matter if you are in the middle of the pack and you report your company's data point at "20.65" or "20.7." In many cases, simply reporting "21" would be precise enough if the best are around 30. Your decision on what to do depends on how far you are from the best performance of any company inside or outside the project. If your statistics and narrative clearly identify the gap between yourself and the best-practice benchmark you will have fulfilled your purpose. The entire process of data collection, preparation, and analysis for the Sample Company is summarized in Exhibit 5.2. The steps followed by this fictitious firm demonstrate how the procedure should flow.

Once you know your company's position compared to the placement of your partners and the best in the area under study, you need to know one more thing. How did the difference develop? What do the best do that you don't do, or vice versa? Do your opportunities for improvement reside with employee skills and attitudes, with process flow, with technological deficiencies, or with organizational structure and policy problems? These are the questions that the evaluation phase in Chapter Six will answer.

Conclusion

The data management phase is the most fun of the whole benchmarking project. This is when you make contact with your benchmarking partners and share data. Your interpersonal skills now come into play. Interviewing is the key skill in this phase. Good interviewers are good listeners. If your contact people don't have strong skills in this area they need to be trained before they waste their time and the time of your benchmarking partners.

Developing questions is an art form and putting them into a survey document is a science. How the questions are phrased

Exhibit 5.2. The Sample Company Staff Benchmarking Project: Phase II. Data Management.

---

1. *Develop a list of questions.*
   a. Sample's team reviews the purpose of the project. What questions would they like to have answers to that would reveal the practices of the best operators in accounts receivable (A/R)?
   b. Team makes a list of questions.
   c. Team checks the questions. Can they answer those about Sample's organization? If so, what value would the answers add?

   (Presume here that they have conducted a review of their process and concluded an internal benchmarking project.)

2. *Select a data collection method and schedule the contact.*
   a. Will Sample use a survey questionnaire, telephone interview, site visit, focus group, or some combination of these methods?
   b. As a result of qualifying calls by the A/R manager and senior accountant Smith, five benchmarking partners have been obtained. They agree on a schedule for the data collection method (telephone interviews) they decided to use.
   c. The project portfolio is prepared and sent with a cover letter from the A/R manager to each of the five benchmarking partners.

3. *Send questions to your partner (if they weren't included in the project portfolio) and carry out the data collection.*
   a. Sample's team makes the contact and collects the data. The decision is made that the contact will be initially by telephone two weeks after the partners have received and had time to review the questions. The contacts are made by the manager of A/R and the two senior accountants.
   b. The data are returned to the project leader who assumed responsibility for collecting and summarizing it.
   c. A full team preliminary review reveals certain points that need to be clarified. Assignments are given to construct a one-sheet form/questionnaire and mail it to the partners after first calling to alert them.

   (Other follow-up methods could be chosen, for example, a site visit.)

4. *Organize and analyze the data.*
   a. The manager and accountants review the data after receiving the second-round responses, applying their professional knowledge to evaluating the findings.
   b. The project leader acts as a process monitor. He or she listens and questions, pointing out how the data can be plumbed for greatest yield and making certain that the data needed to identify best practices have been obtained.
   c. The project leader and accounts receivable manager agree that they will work together to prepare a report for the chief financial officer, controller, and sales manager.

---

and what forms of response you request can restrict the range of possible answers. The form of the questions can also prejudice the answers. If you don't have survey specialists on staff it will be well worth your time to have an outside expert help you. Keep your questions focused on the process or practice being benchmarked. Ask only questions that will yield some value. Ask yourself how you would use the answer to each question. At the same time, be sure that you can answer the questions that you will be asking your partners. You should collect your internal data before you contact benchmarking partners. Running your questions internally first may produce some insights that might even make the benchmarking project unnecessary.

Alert your partners with a precontact package, a project portfolio. The package should contain everything that will help the partner prepare to share relevant data. This preparation saves time, avoids surprises, and is a courteous gesture. You should also prepare partners for any sensitive issues having to do with data disclosure, handling of proprietary information, or ethics. Assembling a project portfolio is an effective method of preparation.

Although data collection often takes much more time and effort than you had imagined, the process is largely enjoyable. The method you select will be determined by the time and money you have to spend and the scope of the project. If you are going to benchmark the practices and processes of an entire unit, such as data operations, you will use a different method from the one that would be appropriate for looking at only one aspect of one process, such as report distribution. Each method has its strong and weak points. Learn what they are before you select one.

If you approach the contact with a positive, learning and listening-rather-than-telling attitude, you can expect cooperation. Be thorough but not pushy in your questioning. Respect your partner's needs and restrictions. Approach your partner as you would a close, long-term friend and you may come out with one. The hard work comes when you have to format and summarize the data, so make this phase as easy as possible by doing a thorough and accurate job of data collection. To help ensure thorough data collection is the reason I suggested having a structured interview form that everyone on the team uses. The person who later tries to summarize the data and make some sense of it will be much more successful if the input is all organized the same way. Be as certain as you can about the relevance, completeness, and accuracy of the information. An ounce of planning will save a ton of trouble later. You'll thank yourself for being so well organized when you are facing a mountain of data.

Data organization involves pulling all the information together and formatting it for evaluation and eventually a project report. The best rule is to keep it simple, brief, and to the point while still covering all key matters. Here is a short checklist:

- Are your data relevant to the questions you started with?
- Are they as complete as possible, given the resources you were able to commit?
- Did any key question slip through the cracks?
- Did the answer to one question raise another that you hadn't thought of and did that get answered?
- Do you have any concerns about the accuracy of the data?

As you prepare the information for a report, keep in mind how you might arrange it in outline form, using graphics and highlighting to make it easy to read. The presentation of findings will be covered in detail in Chapter Six.

6

Evaluation: Developing Strategies for Closing Critical Performance Gaps

The objective of benchmarking is not only to learn how the best organizations conduct certain processes but to close the gap between your performance level and theirs. To accomplish this, your benchmarking project should yield data that answer three questions: (1) What is the benchmark organization doing — step by step — in that process? (2) How are they doing it? (3) Why are they doing it that way?

This chapter deals with the one central issue: finding and closing the gap between your organization's performance and the performance of the target or best practice organization. To evaluate the gap, you have to look at two points in time. First, the gap reflects the differences at the time the data were collected. What is the gap and why does it exist? If your research was complete, you also gathered trend data; this gives you a view into the future and leads to the second point. What will the gap look like in the future? The ever-present and absolutely critical questions are what is the current value or importance of the gap and what is the likelihood that the gap will be meaningful at some future time? Knowing these facts and having made these projections the obvious question is, how will you close the gap?

There are four steps to evaluating and closing the gap:

1.   Locate the gap.
2.   Understand and interpret the gap.
3.   Project and calculate the gap's value into the future.
4.   Develop a change in strategy to close the gap.

In the simplest sense, defining the gap is easy. It involves identifying the difference between your result and the benchmark. The chief caution is to make sure that there is consistency between your internal data and the data collected from your benchmark partners. For the sake of discussion, I will assume that the benchmark is the performance of one of your partners. This is not always true if you are looking for the best practice. When you reach this stage you might believe that the best is yet to be discovered. That does not mean you failed. The gap between yourself and the best in the benchmark project may be sufficient to provide you with your first benchmark.

Typically Ltd. is an excellent example in that it deals with multiple process problems among the several staff units and shows the loss of value that these process problems are causing— the growing market-share gap. Logically, if each staff unit benchmarks its processes and improves its outputs, the collective gain will help the sales force sell easier, sell more, and maybe even obtain higher margins.

You may find at the end of the data phase that your organization looks good compared to your benchmarking partners'. You may even discover that your rate of improvement is greater than theirs. If so, congratulations. Now, it is time to go back to work and find someone who is better than you. I believe that *one* company is going to be the model of best practice; however, the odds are that someone from another company is reading this book right now. Therefore, what comes next is relevant to every reader, perhaps save one.

It is possible but not likely that the performance of your business unit is quite far below the performance level of the best company in your project. This is good to know, although it may not make a lot of people happy. After all, you wanted to know where you stand or you would not have launched this project, right? Let's say that hypothetically your group's performance is 35 percent behind the record of the best company in your project. That is a pretty large gap to close. Nevertheless, your people probably can see themselves closing the gap on a 30 percent differential. But if you were to find that the best company's record was 80 percent better than your performance, which is possible, the news would be quite discouraging. Your staff might feel that they could never catch up with the best. What do you do then to stimulate them to take on the challenge?

One of the secrets to success is constant small improvements. If your group can set a goal of closing 30 percent of the 80 percent gap and do it in a year or so, they will feel very proud of themselves. At that time you can conduct another benchmarking project and see how far you are from the very best. The gap between your unit and the best at that point probably will be much less than 80 percent. It is more difficult for the best to maintain the gap since they have already organized to eliminate most of their large inefficiencies or expenses. They might even have slipped a little. This means you could be less than 50 percent behind. Having experienced some success, your group may have developed the self-confidence, based on their gains of the past year, to take on the best. They might be motivated to try to close 75 percent of the remaining gap within the next year and 100 percent in two years. As the saying goes, nothing succeeds like success!

Many of the companies featured in well-publicized success stories took several years to reach their goals. In cases where systemwide changes had to be made, reaching the goals has required as many as ten years. In the 1970s, Bob Galvin, chairman of Motorola, introduced participative management into that company, but almost a decade elapsed before the practice had spread throughout the company. The lesson is that big changes take lots of time. Sometimes it takes more time than the company has and the enterprise eventually fails. However, in most cases the outcomes are less dramatic. If you can energize the company to take on the challenge and to work at it consistently through continuous improvement you have an excellent chance for success.

Locating the Gap

What is the gap? The difference in performance between your organization and the best-practice target is the gap. The Typically Ltd. example, described in Chapter One, has many potential gaps. The major one is the loss of market share. This is the business problem that stimulated the benchmarking projects in the various staff functions. If benchmarking the staff unit processes fails to contribute to regaining market share, then what is the reason for doing it? Benchmarking may reveal many small but interrelated inefficiencies that together could greatly affect the company's market share. Indeed, the drop in sales seems to have been caused by a combination of problems within and among staff departments. Table 6.1 illustrates the types of gaps that benchmarking could uncover.

The metrics in Table 6.1 illustrate how a problem in one department causes problems in another department or departments. In this "typical" case, solving a process problem in one department will affect how another department functions. The discussion at the meeting, described in Chapter One, told us how the process problem in one department was driven by late or

Table 6.1. Typically Ltd.'s Gaps.

Function	Process	Typically Ltd.'s Performance	Best Practice Performance	Gap
Accounting	Billing errors	5%	.04%	4.5%
Customer Service	Account data	24 hour lag	2.5 hour lag	21.5 hours
Human Resources	Requisition approval	5–6 weeks	1–2 days	4.4 weeks minimum
MIS	Data errors	4%	1%	3%
Procurement	Purchase order processing	3 days	1.5 days	1.5 days
Shipping	Shipment status	8 hour lag	2 hour lag	6 hours

erroneous input from another department or departments. Clearly, organizations are interdependent systems. Benchmarking projects often find that the solution to one functional problem requires cooperation or change in another function.

Understanding and Interpreting the Gap

The key issue in benchmarking is learning. You have learned how big the gap is. The more important information to learn is the reason for the gap. What do the best do differently from what your group does? What are the drivers of their performance? In Chapter Four, I discussed the macro performance drivers and divided them into internal organizational drivers and external environmental ones. Exhibit 6.1 further defines the drivers in the format of an annotated checklist.

As you are collecting data, these factors should be kept in mind. You need to see, hear, and sense them. Some combination of these factors is the force that has created the gap between your unit's performance and the benchmark. If you have conducted the investigation with care, followed proven procedures, and kept your eyes and ears open, you will have the information you need to determine the causes that created the gap. If, when you have finished the job and calculated the gap, you don't know what the causes might be, there is probably something missing or wrong with your data. At the very least you should have a clear sense of the performance drivers that created the gap. You might not know quantitatively which driver offers the greatest value at this point. In Typically Ltd.'s case, which would you work on first?

Masking Performance Gap Drivers

There are several potential reasons for your not being able to identify the gaps. The most common is data problems.

Data Problems. On the one hand, your data may not be complete or accurate. You may need to redo part of the investigation to improve the validity of your information. This is usually

Exhibit 6.1. Checklist of Performance Drivers.

Internal Organizational Drivers

Culture: values, norms, and expectations regarding how hard people work, how they work together, what is acceptable, what is rewarded and what is punished, leadership style, concern for employee safety and security, and so on

Growth: size, profitability, and rate of growth of the organization

Products/Services: type, number, and mix of products and services

Resources: work force (number, cost, motivation, skills, involvement, and decision-making authority), facilities (maintenance of a safe, secure, and efficient physical workplace), and materials (availability of tools, supplies, and raw materials)

Structure: process steps, work rules, reporting lines, control and reward systems, administrative support, geographic dispersion of business units, and so on

Vision: strategic purpose, policies, and plans for the enterprise

External Environmental Drivers

Industry: general trends and conditions as well as practices peculiar to the industry

Information: availability of required data

Location: geographic regional conditions and characteristics where the company's operations are located

Market Forces: local and national economic and social conditions

Regulations: local and national laws, rules, and regulations governing the business operation and product distribution

Technology: availability and applciation of state-of-the-art equipment and knowledge

---

not difficult. By now you have established a relationship with your partners and they won't mind spending a few more minutes with you on the phone to sharpen the data. It is in their best interests to help ensure that the data are as good as they can be. Since the partners will receive a copy of the data you develop, they will want it to be as representative of the benchmarking group as is reasonably possible.

One common data deficiency occurs when your partners don't have good metrics to demonstrate that their process is the best. This lack is not uncommon for staff functions. Their process might feel very good and make a lot of intuitive sense to you, but you may see that they have not done a great job of measuring their performance before you began asking for hard figures. They might have only a few months of metrics that your questions drove them to collect. In these cases you can go with what you have or agree that for the foreseeable future you will all collect and share metrics.

On the other hand, data can be worried to death. There is no need to massage data to three decimal points when no value is to come from it. Insecure people never want to finish manipulating data because they never feel it is precise enough. The psychology behind this is a fear of making decisions and producing a report that others can study and use as a reason for taking action. This fear of commitment manifests itself in the phenomenon commonly known as analysis paralysis. So long as people can busy themselves playing with the data they have an excuse for not doing something with it. Keep in mind the earlier point about the nature of business research. You are not conducting clinical trials for a new drug. You don't have to prove anything at the .001 level. Precision is not the issue. What you need is valid, reasonably accurate information that people can accept. From that, you and others can make decisions, act, and monitor the results of the action.

Misdirection. Another common cause of masked performance drivers is a misdirected project. It might have been flawed from the start. The team may have wanted to investigate, for instance, the cultivation of oranges and production of orange juice. However, in the planning stage they made a fallacious assumption and started down the wrong path. At the end of the data phase they are at a loss to understand what they see before them because they are standing in the middle of a grove of tangerine trees. A variation of misdirection is to start well but get lost along the way. Somehow, somewhere, they get off track and end up studying tangerines. Tangerines are close to oranges. They are both citrus and both orange in color, but tangerines are not oranges. So the benchmarkers will not be able to understand their data when they try to relate it to orange production.

For example, in the case of Typically Ltd., a project within the procurement function could evaluate the work-flow process while ignoring completely the signs that the problem is employee-rather than system-based. Perhaps the supervisor of a key section has so alienated the employees that they are slacking off and letting errors go through so that management will wake up and deal with the supervisor. The process is fine. It could be more efficient if the people wanted it to be. Once you start benchmarking, you never know where the process will take you and you have to keep your blinders off so that you pick up all the signals coming in.

Data Analysis. Another problem has to do with the inability of the benchmark team to understand the data they have. Many people are not very adept at data analysis. This is particularly true when it comes to identifying causal or correlational factors. This deficiency should have been remedied at the beginning through training. However, during fifteen years of teaching people how to handle data, the Saratoga Institute has come across a great number of people who think they know how but don't. We have been publishing annual reports on human resource data since the mid 1980s and we know that some people have bought the report every year and never opened it. They know that they have something of value but they don't know how to read it. I think they buy it as a security blanket. If someone ever asks them for data on the factors we report, they will have it.

More than one benchmarking project has foundered because of deficient data interpretation. I can't emphasize enough the need for benchmarkers to be trained in basic data analysis. Data analysis is such a complex subject that a thorough explication of it is well beyond the scope of this chapter. Practically any type of qualitative or quantitative data can be analyzed for intrinsic and relational insights. Data analysis in benchmarking is mostly a matter of performance and process-structure assessment. Some of the best material for understanding human to human, and human to process-system interfaces came out of group dynamics work done in the 1930s. In the late 1960s and early 1970s this seminal work reemerged as what came to be called *organization development.* Two of the many books that laid a foundation for work analysis were Schein's *Process Consultation* (1969) and Mager and Pipe's *Analyzing Performance Problems* (1970).

More recently there has been a resurgence in process improvement driven by the quality gurus. The work of Deming (1986), Juran (1988), and Crosby (1984), as well as Harrington's *Business Process Improvement* (1991) provide an excellent self-study course in problem identification and data analysis. You can find examples of everything from flowcharts and checklists through Pareto diagrams and force-field analysis to statistical procedures such as histograms and scattergrams.

As I mentioned earlier, engineers in the production end of the business know how to deal with quantitative data. But this is most often not true in staff functions. Even in information services, which is populated with systems people who are math wizards, the ability to use this type of operational or managerial accounting data is often lacking. There is more to it than knowing how to run esoteric regression statistics. Your team will need to be able to feel the data. That is, they will have to be able to scan tables or graphs and see patterns. This skill comes from practice. They will need an appreciation for the natural interaction between outcomes. For example, there is a correlation between hiring and turnover data, between turnover and absenteeism, between operator training and production results, and between sales volume, accounts receivable, and cash balances. When I say this, you may reply that of course everyone knows that. However, in practice, I have seen many professionals and managers whose eyes glaze over and whose expressions go blank when the discussion turns to actual analysis of quantitative data.

If you lack the ability to grasp the hidden relationships of data, benchmarking becomes a futile and potentially misleading exercise. Nevertheless, although analysis is sometimes difficult, it is not mystical. Display techniques such as matrices and line charts can reveal the relationships that narrative does not yield. Table 6.1 is an example of a simple comparative display.

It will be difficult in the next step to project a gap several years into the future if you do not truly understand its causes or have historic data to support your claim. The future is obscured when there is no knowledge of the past. Many benchmarking projects, particularly administrative process investigations, do not have a data history. They are different from sales and production in this regard. Because administrative groups have been allowed to sidestep performance measurement for decades, they often do not have any data on process efficiency. If, however, you don't have internal data on your own work, you may be able to draw on industry or professional data bases for historic data. As I mentioned earlier, the Saratoga Institute has been publishing data on processes such as hiring, benefit costs, compensation programs, and training since 1986. These provide a baseline that clients can use to project the movement of these processes within their industry, section of the country, or companies of their size. Data are also available from the U.S. Chamber of Commerce, Bureau of National Affairs, Commerce Clearing House, groups such as American Productivity and Quality Center, and American Society for Quality Control, as well as from many trade and professional associations, and local and federal government bureaus.

   In the absence of reliable historic data you do the best you can. Talk with your benchmarking partners. They may have sources. Did you ask them for historic data along the way? If you didn't cover it the first time around, you can certainly go back and ask for it now. You might offer to project the gap of the group mean or even individual companies against the best-practice company. You will need trend data from the past to do that.

Key Questions

There are two questions relevant to understanding a gap: What is the gap? Why is there a gap? One is the result; the other is the cause of the differences. As you gather data, you will be asking your partners what they are doing, and more importantly, why are they doing it that way? If you collect only the *what*, you will be on your own when you try to figure out *why* they are better than you, if they are. Even when they aren't better, it is useful to know why they chose to construct their process the way they did. Usually there is a rationale that goes into the design of a work process. The reason may be lost in antiquity.

That is, they may say they have always done it that way and they never thought to question it. We can hope, however, that they have given it some thought and can tell you why the process is the way it is. Let me reemphasize: *Why* is as important as *What*!

The answer to the *why* question is found in such areas as available technology; work rules; organizational policy and culture; employee skills, attitudes, and motivations; managerial preferences; or any of the performance drivers listed in Exhibit 6.1. It is the influence of these drivers in your partners' organizations that make it impossible for you to achieve good results through imitation. The mix of driving forces is different in each organization. But if you see how they mix, you may see why your partner's forces are better than yours. Then you can adapt whatever is useful for your own process.

When Americans first became enamored with Japanese quality programs, they tried to bring them into American companies in the same form as they were applied in Japan. For the most part the results were not satisfactory. In some cases they bombed completely. The reason was that American consultants and managers ignored the key driver of the Japanese quality method, which was the consensual nature of Japanese culture. The new world ideal of individualism and egalitarianism is diametrically opposite the consensus model.

As you are gathering data, use all your senses. Do more than listen intently. Look, taste, and smell what is going on. You know what I mean. Get underneath the obvious to feel the nature of the organization. Continually ask yourself, why? What is really happening here? Why does it make sense for them to do it that way? Is it the volume, the demand for speed or quality? Is it the way they view their employees? Is there an autocratic, democratic, or laissez-faire style of management operating? Who decided that the process should run this way? What kinds of stresses does it induce or eliminate? Processes and practices are often driven more by invisible than by visible factors. In Chapter Nine I will describe the hidden driving forces discovered in a best practice study of 110 companies.

In summary, there are positive and negative considerations in gap projection. Both are critical; neither can be ignored. One will support you; the other will inhibit you. If you have enough valid, accurate current data, historic trend data, skills in data interpretation, and an understanding of the driving forces that caused your partners to design their processes the way they did, you will be in position to project. Then, if you do not submit to data analysis paralysis and do not lose your focus during the investigation, you will be well on your way to being able to complete the task accurately.

Projecting and Calculating the Gap

Let's assume you know the *what* and the *why* that explains the gap.

1. You asked the why and the how questions during your benchmarking interviews.
2. You also gathered recent history and past trend data.
3. You identified the performance drivers and have correctly interpreted the data.
4. As a result you know where you are and in which direction you are moving at what speed. That is, you know your current rate of improvement or degradation. You know the same thing about the best-practice target company.

When you know position, direction, velocity, and time, it is a simple matter to calculate any future position. You can predict the gap yourself and the target at any point in the future.

The National Aeronautics and Space Administration (NASA) followed this procedure when they planned and prepared for the launch that put the American Eagle on the moon in 1969. The scientists knew where the earth and the moon were relative to each other in 1960 and where they would be on any given date in the future. They knew the directions and speeds at which both bodies were moving. From this they could calculate vectors or courses based on the best time to launch the astronauts, assuming a given speed of the spacecraft. The complication was that the earth and the moon were moving in elliptical orbits. If they had been moving in parallel lines any school child with basic arithmetic skills could have predicted the contact point.

Projecting your gap is much more difficult. While NASA knew that their speed and direction factors were 100 percent predictable, you don't have that comfort. It is easier to predict the position of the moon at any given point in the future relative to the earth than it is to predict the future market position of any company. Business does not run on the laws of astronomy and physics. Experience has shown that business decisions are sometimes more dependent on the desires of the CEO's spouse to live in a given city than on the economics of locating the business there. (I personally know two cases where that was the deciding factor.)

Since your projection must be made in a world of change rather than constancy, you have to estimate future directions and velocities. The last thing to ask yourself before you project the gap is this: What is the rate and direction of improvement of the best practice target? How sure are you?

The next obvious question is this: According to your calculations and estimations, is the gap widening or closing between you and your target if both continue at the present direction and velocity? How far into the future will you project? You can pick multiple points — one year, three years, five years. If no change occurs in either company, what will be the gap at each point in the future? What improvements in speed and direction would it take on your part to close that gap 100 percent within one, three, or five years?

You might also project alternative scenarios featuring different rates of direction and speed. You want to offer more than one vector on your intercept graph. It gives management choices. If the target is operating at an extremely high rate of efficiency, it is very difficult for that company to make major improvements in the future. For example, Motorola set 6 sigma as their target for quality, as illustrated in Figure 6.1. A sigma is one standard deviation from the mean. Six sigma means that their quality target is to have fewer than three product defects per million parts manufactured. Motorola has been able to

Figure 6.1. Intercept Graph.

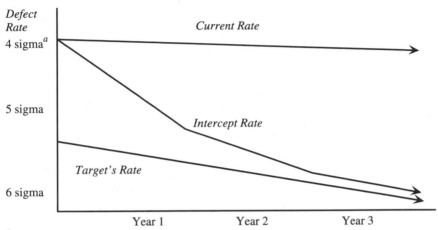

*A sigma is one standard deviation from the mean.

achieve this extremely high level of quality in some of their manufacturing. If you consider Motorola your competition and are operating at 4 sigma, your people are allowing more than five thousand defects per million parts. It will be much easier for you to bring your defect rate down to near 6 sigma than it is for Motorola to reduce theirs to less than one defect per million. Therefore, you might project Motorola's improvement rate as a fractional percentage and yours at 50 percent in one year, another 30 percent in the second year, with the goal of being at 6 sigma in no more than three years. This would leave the gap so small as to be indistinguishable by the customer. Of course, a company as good as Motorola is not going to wait for you. It will be looking for other ways to maintain a competitive edge.

Benchmarking projects usually do not require massive change. However, large-scale, organizationwide benchmarking is driven by the need to make massive change as quickly as possible. In such broad-based efforts, you can anticipate the most virulent resistance to change. In order to make change happen you have to persuade people that the change will make things better, and you must involve them as participants in the change. Of course, if I am going to lose my job as a result of the changes you suggest, you're in for a hard sell. No one likes to have change done to him or her. Your only chance for full acceptance is involvement.

When you present your findings and projections with an intercept graph, people can easily see what is most likely to happen based on your data, which incidentally is the best data on hand at the moment. This is the point at which personal and organizational resistance to change begins to solidify. The way you present your arguments in the report, which we will discuss in Chapter Seven, will have a great deal to do with your ability to obtain commitment. It is easy for people to support a benchmarking project in the beginning. However, when they are asked to review data that upsets their views and threatens their positions, their defensive behavior is predictable.

Developing a Change Strategy

Benchmarking presumes continuous change and improvement. The key issues with continuous improvement are participation and value adding. Talk of employee participation has been around since the 1950s with the advent of the human relations movement. At that time, the concept was that employees should be given a sense of participation in the decision making of the organization. As it turned out, that is exactly what employees got: a "sense" of participation. They quickly learned they were being duped and opted out of the movement. Over the years, other employee-involvement programs have come and gone. Now, *empowerment* is the key term. Whatever it is called, employee involvement must be present and must be real if a company is to improve. This means that some portion of the work force must be involved with benchmarking. Therein lies a potential pitfall. If management is not on top of the program, a lot of benchmarking projects will be undertaken just because they are supposed to be. A giant activity trap lies alongside the road to Kaizen. Avoid running a project that yields limited returns. Don't trade activity for true value.

The second point of continuous, or for that matter any, improvement is that the only way to make any idea last in an organization is to institutionalize it. It must become part of the day-to-day system of management. There must be reward when it is carried out and punishment when it is neglected. Chapter Nine provides an example of what I mean about systemization. The best-practice companies have institutionalized the nine best-practice values, strategies, and traits defined in that chapter. Communication, for example, is not something that is done periodically. It is a process as systematized as financial reporting. Interdependence is not a concept. It has been institutionalized with regular interdepartmental meetings.

Institutionalizing training means that training and retraining are part of everyone's career. Instead of being sent to a periodic training program for some haphazard reason, everyone participates in regularly scheduled programs. *Continuous learning* is a better term because that is what it is. Training is a program. Career development is a system. Change augmented by career development has a better chance of working.

Nevertheless, systemic change can be traumatizing. Trying to revamp the entire organization in one fairly quick stroke is extremely difficult. My experience is that challenging interim targets should be set, achieved, and built on. This approach has a much higher chance of success. As changes are made they must be institutionalized or they will fade away when you turn your attention to the next target. The institutional imperative requires a company to prepare itself for continuous improvement through a true value-adding work program rather than a series of projects whose results have short lives.

You must decide what is realistic in terms of your company's ability to make changes and quickly close a gap. Can it be accomplished within one year, two, three? Realism brings into play your company's internal and external performance drivers. If the gap is not wide, the changes are not great, resistance is minimal, and there are no extraneous forces impinging on management, your company may choose to attempt the entire change in one year. On the other hand, although the desire might be there and resistance might be minimal, the necessary resources might not be available. Strategic imperatives such as a major restructuring or downsizing may absorb everyone's time for the next eighteen months. Stockholders may be pressuring top management for improved profits, and their demands could preclude a significant investment in new technology at this time. The logical, long-term solution is not always the course that is chosen. The battle is one of sometimes conflicting values. All this and more needs to be considered as you map your strategy for presenting your case for change.

Change Tactics

You can refer to a number of tactics in planning how to recommend change in your benchmarking project report. One approach is to look back at the nine reasons for resisting change (first introduced in Fitz-enz, 1991), and turn them into a checklist for approaching change. Exhibit 6.2 is an annotated list of barriers to change. If you know the enemy, you've won the first half of the battle. Although the nine points are listed separately you will find that there are very close relationships between many of them. Don't worry about the nomenclature or format. Just look for solutions to the resistance factors.

In addition to the nine human resistance factors, change can also be limited by time and amount of change. The amount of time that will be required to make and institutionalize the changes will affect your chances for success. People are busy and easily distracted. This is why a series of small changes is easier than one big long-term project. Improvement can also be curtailed by the scope and complexity of the change—that is, the number of people or groups affected and the number of changes attempted. Finally, the degree of difficulty is directly dependent on the amount of change that will be caused in operational or social systems. Any time you have to disrupt a system you will find that resistance increases in proportion to the size of the system. It is harder to knock down a cement wall than a picket fence. Once again, unless you have a bulldozer, it is easier and more effective to chip away at a huge wall until enough of the foundation is removed that it falls of its own weight.

Exhibit 6.2. Barriers to Change.

---

1. *Homeostasis.* Homeostasis is based on insecurity. Which individuals currently seem the least secure personally or might be most changed by the recommendations you will make? List groups and individuals. What will the change mean to them? What can you build in that will provide psychological security?

2. *Habit.* Habits threaten competence. Will the changes in practices or process require giving up old skills and learning new ones? Changing from one set of forms to another is not a threat to competence. Shifting from a manual to an automated system is. Should you look into training requirements and build that into your report?

3. *Perception.* Until previously unseen, unfelt needs are perceived you will have difficulty gaining support for change, and reality can be unpleasant. Will you have to confront someone or some group that believes there is no problem? The "Z" chart is a quick way to show the problem (see Figure 2.2 on page 31 as an example). Then, follow up with the cost of the gap and reinforce the point that the best-practice firm is comparable to yours.

4. *Dependence.* Yes, it might be nice to have some of the good old-fashioned values operating today. Values are most often found in practices. It's the "we've always/never done it that way" defense. Moving toward empowerment and participation may conflict with old autocratic values. Try to couch your recommendations in ways that do not directly confront old values. Focus instead on the problem and show how the new practice is more suitable for the situation.

5. *Regression.* The past is past. What worked then was suitable for those conditions. Today, your company faces new problems. The solution to every problem is found within the problem. We can't overcome new problems by working harder at them with old tools. So, present the new tools along with the problem and the solution.

6. *Norms.* Norms — the proper way to do things — lead to beliefs of uniqueness. The attitude is, "We're different so we do things this way." Your data will show comparability by matching up performance drivers. Furthermore, it will show the constraints that are self-imposed. Showing that you measure up well with the best-practice company should encourage the doubters to believe they can make the change.

7. *Vested Interests.* Will your recommendations affect anyone's power base? If your organization realizes that the new base of power should be value-added results rather than the generation of expensive fiefdoms, you won't have a problem. Nevertheless, someone is likely to be bruised in the change and you need to prepare for that.

8. *Rituals and Taboos.* Are any of the old procedures threatened? You may have to replace some old ceremonies, such as methods of recognition, with new ones. They may not be very visible or meaningful to you, but they can be very important to others.

9. *Rejection of the Outside.* Benchmarking data are usually pretty effective with this resistance point. The first counterpoint is to show comparability in performance drivers between your firm and the benchmark firm. That should

Exhibit 6.2. Barriers to Change, Cont'd.

---

demonstrate that the other process can work here. Next, point out the constraining factors that are keeping your firm from matching up to the best-practice company. Focus on process and value added rather than on persons and problems. This approach should help defuse the not-invented-here factor.

Reviewing Value Added

Herein lies the core issue: what is the value to be gained or lost from taking on the change effort and closing or not closing the gap? In the case of Typically Ltd., the value was regaining market share. In Chapter One, I made a strong case for value being the driving force in benchmarking. This is another reason for being value focused. The only justification for mobilizing resources to launch a benchmarking project is to reach a specific, identifiable value goal. You kept in mind as you planned the project that there would be certain values obtained for the company and for the customer if you could significantly improve the process or practice you were benchmarking. What were these values? Do you still believe in them? Do you need to adjust them based on what you know now?

It is not uncommon at this point to make a major decision based on new data. You would expect that with all the information you have collected your initial views could be altered. For instance, you might now see much more or much less value in making the improvements you had in mind at the start. This usually won't happen if you are benchmarking some administrative process. But in extreme cases where data are being collected on something like product marketing, it could prompt management to develop new product or market-penetration strategies. You could find that the differences are so great that it might make more sense to abandon one market niche for another. In that case, certain operational procedures within marketing may no longer be appropriate.

As you view the performance gap, what is the value inherent in the deficiency? That is, what competitive advantage are you giving up presently? Might it have an impact on the unit cost of products or services? If so, how much? Does it inhibit the ability of the sales force to sell because of time delays in delivery? If so, how much difference could it make if deliveries were shortened? In *2020 Vision,* Stan Davis and Bill Davidson (1991, p. 58) commented on the delivery time of Hino Motors, a Japanese truck manufacturer. Hino can produce over 1,900 different truck configurations within an average lead time of just five days. That must be a great competitive advantage.

The issue of value is the pivotal point. It was so at the time you considered benchmarking and it is still true when you have completed the data gathering. When you prepare your report, focus on the quantifiable values, the competitive edge that the changes will yield for your organization.

Exhibit 6.3 presents the evaluation process as it might unfold for the fictitious Sample Company. The use of actual quantitative data here helps you get a feel for the reality of evaluation.

Conclusion

Benchmarking is about learning, and it is during the evaluation phase that the learning comes into focus. Handle the data carefully. Is the information valid? Does it measure what you think it measures? Is it consistent? When you look at patterns within the data do they come together in a congruent picture? Make sure that you have the skills on the team to comprehend and work with the data. Watch and listen as your team discusses the findings. Do they understand what they have? Can they turn the data into a concise and compelling report? Will they be able to answer questions? Nothing is so embarrassing as not being able to field questions from management when you present the report.

Because no one truly knows the future, it may be useful to project more than one scenario. The direction and rate of improvement of the target company cannot be known for certain, but what might be the most reasonable vectors, given their competitive position now? Can you close the gap in one big jump over the next year or eighteen months? Or might it be more

Exhibit 6.3. The Sample Company Staff Benchmarking Project: Phase III. Evaluation.

---

1. *Locating the gap*. The gap has been identified. The best-practice companies have an advantage over us in terms of time to prepare invoices, error rates, and aging of accounts receivables. It takes us an average of 8.5 days from the time an order is received to the time it is shipped and the customer's bill (invoice) is prepared. In addition, we are experiencing a 5 percent error factor on shipments and bills. The best practice is 2.5 days from order entry to billing. Their error factor is 0.7 percent. Our average account receivable collection time is fifty-six days. The best-practice time is forty-three days.

2. *Understanding the gap*. It appears that the reason behind our slower billing time has to do with the delays and subsequent errors occurring between order entry, shipping, and accounting. Our process now includes passing duplicate copies of the documents between the departments. There is some double data entry resulting in delays and errors between order entry and shipping, and between shipping and accounts receivable. The best-practice organization has this process automated. In the past, management has refused to automate this process, believing we should be able to solve it in a manual mode first.

3. *Projecting and calculating the gap*. At the rate we and the best-practice benchmark are moving, in two years we will still take more than four days and the best-practice model will take less than one day to process and ship an order. Our error rate will be about 2–3 percent and the best is aiming at 0.25 percent. Our receivable time will be fifty-two days and the best model will be forty-one days.

   Given the average billing per order and the volume of sales and accounts receivable, the team will now calculate the cost of the gap to the company. The cost will be not only the direct cost of money but the projected value of lower customer satisfaction possibly leading to customer loss. In order to determine this last factor, a review of reasons for lost customers in the past year will be made with the marketing department, and the cost of acquiring a customer will be calculated.

4. *Developing a change strategy*. Looking ahead: as we review the data regarding the gaps and the reasons for them, we have to consider the ability of the organization to close the gap. Does the company have the resources and the will to make the changes that will be recommended in our report? What will it take to sell the change? The checklist in Exhibit 6.2 should help answer that question.

---

reasonable to try it over several years? Hewlett-Packard CEO John Young once told me that he proposed a ten-year plan to close the gap on one basic operating factor.

Try to determine the capacity of your organization to absorb change. What are the key resistance factors? Who might be the primary resistors? Look at your task from the standpoint of supporting and inhibiting forces. Who will you have to persuade? What are the most persuasive points for each of those people?

Finally, when you have identified and quantified the value of the gap, show both sides. This is what you get if you close the gap. This is what you lose if you don't close the gap. Express the gap in terms of dollar value: expense level, market share sales, profit. Everyone understands money.

I believe that benchmarking is an art form. To use the terminology of art, the gap is the figure and the issues surrounding it are the ground. The size and value of the gap are the key issues; the reasons for it, and the company's capacity to change and close the gap, are the background.

Success in implementing large-scale change through benchmarking is most often achieved through patience. The notion of continuous improvement is built on the principle of small, consistent success. It is the way you build self-esteem and self-confidence in people, and people are what make the organization successful. Build a strong case for the changes required. Then, make them in small, determined, incremental steps as fast as the organization can handle the changes.

7

Action:
Gaining Commitment to Change

*At this point something has to happen. You need ac-
tion. This is where communication becomes important
again. You had to communicate and persuade all
through the project. Now, your success will be determined by two factors: (1) how effective a sales person
you are, and (2) how well you lead the change effort.
In the latter case you may not have to be the hands-on
leader, but if you're not, you have to convince someone
else to take on the role.*

Action is triggered by communication. Nothing
happens until you have presented your data to your internal
customers and gained their commitment to doing something with
it. Each step in the benchmarking process is important, but none
is more important than obtaining commitment or "making the
sale." Success is not a function of having a great product. Success is a result of selling the product. Accountants will try to
tell you that inventory is an asset. I can testify as a business
owner who has to personally finance his inventory, it is a liabil-
ity until someone buys it. You don't want to work for months
and then have your recommendations rejected. Your project
may have great intrinsic merit but it will become an asset only
when someone buys in to using your data and making positive
change in your organization.

Communication is the key skill in obtaining a commitment to action. There are four steps in the action phase:

150

1. Preparing to report
2. Structuring the report
3. Driving toward the goals
4. Planning and leading change

Three of these steps require communication. The first two deal with communicating findings and making recommendations. In the last step, planning and leading change, you obviously need to be persuasive.

Communicating and benchmarking are inseparable. Most of the work in a benchmarking project is devoted to communicating. Your time is spent developing questions, asking questions, answering questions and sharing data, and finally, preparing and delivering a report. It will be useful to review effective elements of communications as they relate to your project report. These elements will provide a solid base on which to build your reporting process.

Communication Imperatives

The following four imperatives form the foundation on which rests your success in communicating your benchmarking project report:

1. *Understanding.* Present the data in clear, concise terms so that your audience grasps your key points. You have a very short period of time in the beginning of your presentation, usually less than three minutes, to create interest. The mental and emotional response you seek from your audience is, "This is interesting. I understand what the presenter is saying and showing me."

2. *Overcoming resistance:* Present the data so as to avoid creating defensiveness in your listeners; let your audience see that you are not criticizing them. Here you want your listeners to feel that they are not being attacked, either personally or as a work group. The desired response at this point is between neutral and positive.

3. *Acceptance.* Present the data in a persuasive manner that engenders a sense of commitment and urgency on the part of

your audience. This is sign-up time. This is the point at which buy-in occurs and people are ready to charge out the door motivated to act.

4. *Implementation.* Send the audience away with the data and recommendations they need to initiate the required changes. You need to end the presentation not only by creating a desire in your audience to make change but also by giving them the information tools they need to make it happen.

Persuasion Opportunities

You have three opportunities to sell your ideas and recommendations: before, during, and after the benchmarking project.

1. *Preselling.* It is important to prepare the ground for whatever you want to plant. This means you will be talking with key decision makers before you introduce an idea. You will sound them out and provide information relative to the issue you have in mind. This is often an informal, chatty exchange in which you see into the mind of your audience. You broach the subject, gather information, and prepare yourself to sell later.

2. *Selling.* The main event is the actual selling of your ideas. Here you attempt to persuade your audience to your way of thinking. You allay their fears, make your points, and state the compelling reasoning behind your conclusions. Then, you call for action and ask for commitment.

3. *Reinforcing.* Selling never ends because the world is a dynamic place. You win people to your point of view today, then something happens and tomorrow they start to waver. Your job is like patrolling the dike. You must continually watch for leaks. Small leaks of commitment can one day break the dike and sweep your project away. Stay in contact with the people who are supporting and carrying out the change.

Preparing to Report

I consider report writing to be more than an exercise in information transmission. Reports are opportunities to sell your point of view. This is especially true in benchmarking, where the news is not always welcome.

Knowing Your Audience

The first rule of persuasion or selling is to know your customer. In this case, the customers are the audiences for your report. You may be reporting to top management, which has certain expectations of the function in question; the department head and key reporting personnel, who have created the practices; first-line supervisors and the employees who work the process; or all of the above. Additional interested parties may be stakeholders in other parts of the organization who will be affected by the changes you are recommending. Stakeholders include suppliers to the business unit that runs this process and internal customers for the products and services of the unit. In some cases, outside suppliers and customers may be directly affected by the change. They could be invited to the presentation as well. A decade ago the idea of inviting outsiders into corporate planning meetings was not even considered. Today, it is becoming an accepted notion. In effect, everyone upstream or downstream from the business unit being benchmarked may have an interest in what you have to say. They may also have something of value to offer.

Whether you make oral or written presentations to one individual or to a group, your success will depend on two points. The first has nothing to do with your project but has everything to do with you personally. Selling, or persuasion if you prefer, is an activity that involves two or more human beings. So, the first question is, what is your relationship with your audience? Do they know you? Do they like you, tend to respect and believe you? Or, in the past, have you had some problems with them? You can even be guilty by association. The audience may not know you personally but may have had a bad experience with people from your function or profession. Their distrust may even be based on hearsay. If you are going to present to a group that is disbelieving or even hostile, you are starting with two and a half strikes against you. The first step of report preparation, then, has to do with understanding the relationship between your audience — your customers — and you on a personal level. If there is anything negative between you, clear it up before you try to sell your project to them. This is the preselling

I mentioned above. Remember, people tend to buy more readily from friends than from enemies.

The second basic point of persuasion is to understand your
audience in terms of the subject — the product — you are going
to sell them. What are their interests, values, attitudes, and needs
as these relate to your project and to the processes and practices you benchmarked? Point by point, you can see why these .
are important. If the audience has limited or no interest in the
topic, you will have to tell them in the opening paragraph of
the report or the first sixty seconds of your talk why they should
be interested. It's hard to convince people who are dozing off.
If they are interested, do they see value in the work you are
talking about or in the outcomes of the function? Quite often,
line managers don't see much value in staff work. At best, they
view it as a necessary evil or a hindrance. You want to show
them the connection that runs from the process you have benchmarked all the way to the outside customer. To do this, you
might review the value-added chain described in Chapter Three,
Figure 3.1. The next question is, what is their attitude toward
your topic? Have they had any personal or secondhand experience with it and how do they feel about it? Usually you will
be presenting to someone who is directly involved with the
process/practice or to higher levels of management who over-
see it. Are they happy or not with what has been happening?
Finally, you want to establish a need within them, if it isn't already there, to do what you are suggesting.

Ultimately, what you will sell them is not your recommendations but the values that will flow from the recommendations. No one buys a product or a service. They buy the benefits that the product or service gives them. In this case, the chief
benefit is survival as a viable business on one hand and competitive advantage in the market on the other. In Typically Ltd.'s
case, the chief value was regaining market share. Your values
should encompass as many aspects as possible. Look for cost,
time, quantity, quality, and human values emanating from your
recommendations. Will they improve quality, productivity, and
service? What other values might ensue? This is what your audience really wants to know.

Before you begin to organize your data, focus on your

audience. No matter what the data say or suggest, your success will depend partially on factors outside the data or the project. Build your relationship solidly before presentation time. You could have been preselling all along by keeping key people informed of progress issues with ongoing status reports during the project. You don't have to talk with everyone beforehand if the audience is going to be large, but you do want to have the people who are the leaders, the primary opinion and attitude influencers, on your side. You could have asked them for comments along the way or even made periodic short, informal progress reports. The point is to develop a strategy at the beginning for what you need to do to make a sale at the end.

Choosing Your Methods

The two most common ways to communicate the results of a benchmarking project are by written reports and formal oral presentations. Each has a unique purpose and form. The presentation format often influences acceptance of the data, which are only part of the act. The style of the presentation is equally important. Follow any cultural or procedural style requirements that your organization endorses. If the style fails to capture or even turns off the audience, they will never get past style to substance. You know from your own experience how much more receptive you are to written and oral presentations if they are done well. Lengthy narrative without breaks and illustrations frustrates readers and makes audiences restless. I once followed a speaker at a European management conference in Paris who literally put his audience to sleep. We had just come from the typical five-course French lunch complete with wine, of course. The audience was very relaxed, to say the least. The presenter was somewhat nervous and not very experienced at public speaking. He proceeded to read his speech for over twenty minutes without looking up. The auditorium was filled with six hundred people, some of whom were audibly snoring after the first ten minutes. When he did look up because some who had stayed awake were making noises that indicated their boredom, he said, "I'm not finished," and continued reading for another fifteen minutes. His was a great act to follow.

In addition to formal reports to large groups, you may also be making informal presentations to individuals. These might be either conversational or more structured, such as a presentation to the CEO or a small, top management team. In both cases, the personal issues still apply. Prepare your audience so that when you walk in the door they are interested in what you have to say and are positively predisposed to listening. In this case, timing can be important. Try to schedule the meeting for a time when the person or persons are naturally most receptive. You want to catch your audience when they most likely are not stressed or preoccupied. Sometimes you will have to fit your presentation into a regularly scheduled management meeting. Talk to someone such as the leader's secretary or administrative assistant about the best time for your presentation. They know how the meetings work and they will tell you that you should be on first, last, or somewhere in between.

The site of the presentation is also important. The atmosphere can add to or detract from what you are trying to do. Consider getting your audience out of their offices or conference room to a place where you have more control. You don't want it to be so foreign as to make them feel uncomfortable or threatened, but do you want to be able to control the environment. I have made over five hundred presentations and I always try to meet in a space that lets people feel comfortable and receptive. As silly as it may sound, low-ceilinged rooms are very negative spaces. They are not conducive to openness; they suppress energy and cause people to be impatient. People need space. If your presentation will take more than thirty minutes, they need to be able to move, to slide their chairs around and relieve tension. A little time spent planning the presentation time and site will pay big dividends.

There are other methods for communicating the results of benchmarking projects. Some large companies have established internal benchmarking networks to share data. They publish summaries of methodology, produce newsletters, or generate other forms of communication. The objective is to share information and, more importantly, to gradually make benchmarking a part of the work system. This is the only way that benchmarking will reach its full potential. Putting motivational posters on the wall will not do it. Most people today are sophisticated enough to understand that posters are propaganda. Involving them from the outset of something and making them a part of it will do more to gain commitment than anything we might tell them.

Structuring the Report

The report has two sections: the executive summary and the full report. You know the purposes of each. The summary is for those who are not directly involved in the project or who have only a short time to devote to grasping the purpose and results of the project. Given that most people are hard pressed these days to deal with all the pressures on them, the audience for summaries is growing. Often they read the summary to learn whether the issue is important enough to invest more of their time in it. In light of these constraints, you will want your summary to be a very effective product. It must tell your reader why the benchmark project was important enough for company resources to be spent on it. This is what writers call the "hook." Once you have established the project as an important issue for your reader, you can then go on to report the findings and make your recommendations.

Kami (1988, pp. 174–175) offers several rules of thumb for preparing and selling your proposal. The following are his guidelines:

1. Write in a telegraphic style, without prepositions, adjectives, or excess verbiage.
2. Present everything in priority order.
3. Use quantitative rather than descriptive statements, numbers instead of words wherever possible.
4. State your conclusions and recommendations unequivocally.
5. Offer a list of alternatives for strategy and execution.
6. Prior to the presentation, send your audience the complete package.
7. To capture attention quickly, start by stating the key issue.

Your proposal should address the following questions in the order indicated:

- Why do we need your recommended action? (the problem)
- What will the action accomplish? (the value added)
- How will it be implemented? (the procedure)
- When will it be completed? (the time schedule)
- Who will do it? (the players)
- How much will it cost? (the budget)

Executive Summary

The summary must be concise and clear. It is an outline, not a full exposition. The summary can be structured in several ways. I prefer the following four parts: purpose, findings, recommendations, and process. The reader is focused on the main points rather than being induced to plow through secondary issues covered by the process section. Frankly, you don't want to get into a discussion of methodology, as we will see later.

As a rule of thumb, I try to show both sides of a point. If I say we collected data using telephone interviews rather than on-site visits, I will explain why. I will try to make the case, for instance, that given the time and budget, site visits were not possible. Then, I will explain that telephone interviews were sufficient for the information that we needed to gather. I might say that the nature of the process we were studying was such that viewing it in action would have added very little additional information and would not have contributed to any greater insights. By showing both sides you preempt an objection by making the argument yourself and avoid the classic "Yes, but . . . " reply by explaining why you didn't do the project some other way. In effect you are saying, "We thought of that and discarded it in favor of this choice for these reasons."

Purpose. Why did you undertake this project? What value did you discover that drove you to spend your resources on this topic rather than on another? I find the value-added chain very effective in making this point. Describe briefly how the ultimate value added will improve your competitive position. Explain how it serves the strategic imperatives of the organization.

Findings. The section on findings covers the process or practice that was benchmarked in terms of what you learned. Use both narrative and a few key graphics to illustrate the best practice. Tell how it compares to your current practice. Point out the gap without elaboration. This part has to be written very cleanly. Write as tightly as you possibly can. Focus directly on only the most important points. Those points should be quick highlights: You are trying to capture the excitement of what you learned. Business people like to be excited. They are competitive. Give them the guts of the learning without embellishment. If they want more, they will go into the full report. The combination of the purpose and findings are your selling points. This is where you will capture the imagination and involvement of your audience.

Recommendations. Now, you are ready to set the hook. This is where you present the best practice model. Your recommendations should be quite unequivocal. You tell them what the gap is, why it is where it is, how it got there, and most important, the implications of not closing it. These points should be backed up with references to the value-adding purpose confirmed by the findings. You found such-and-such; therefore, this is what should be done. Say it straightaway. Show the value added, the magnitude of the competitive advantage. Graphs are very effective in this section, so that your audience can see the degree of change that you're talking about.

One point often left out of reports is the downside: what is the likely result of not closing the gap? This projection is what is implied by the trends. The result is not only that you will be X percent behind the competition at the outcome level. You must show the negative effect in terms of impact and value not added if you don't close the gap. For some reason, the negative consequence is often a more effective selling point than the value to be gained.

Your recommendation becomes the de facto model of best

practice for your company. It describes what things will look like when you have made the changes. The model will cover both the quantitative results and the qualitative practices and processes. The quantitative part shows the difference between your company and the best-practice firm. The qualitative part shows the reasons for the differences. The model displays within its recommendations the criteria that define best practice. The following list summarizes the factors you should consider as you prepare your recommendations:

- *Strategic planning methods:* who is involved, how often it's done, and how it's done
- *Communication methods:* the who and how of employee and operational information movement
- *Quantitative and qualitative performance measurement methods:* operating ratios for time, cost, volume, and quality, perhaps accompanied by customer-satisfaction or even employee-attitude measures
- *Reward and recognition systems:* formal and informal methods for rewarding and recognizing excellent performance
- *Operating ratios for quality, productivity, and service:* standards or goals to be achieved to close the gap
- *Management and leadership style:* individual and teamwork factors

In effect, your report will say that if we approach the function in a manner described by the model's criteria, we should realize X results, which will yield Y benefits. Those benefits may be described in both objective and subjective terms. The value of the Y is what the company receives for its efforts. This benefit will be repeated in more detail in the main report.

Process. If you didn't win your audience over with the first three sections, the rest of the summary won't do it for you. This is simply a description of how the project ran. It includes basic data, without elaboration, on the following items:

- *Research:* data sources such as publications, data bases, individuals inside and outside the organization, reverse engineering, and other work done to establish baselines and locate benchmark partners

- *Project team:* a list of the people and their titles who were involved directly, and a list of the indirect support personnel
- *Benchmark partners:* organizations contacted, departments selected, and individuals with whom you met or talked on the telephone; reasons why these organizations/departments were chosen and perhaps why some others that were identified did not qualify or chose not to participate
- *Process:* outline of the steps from the beginning to the end of the project along with a calendar of events and methods employed, such as telephone interviews, site visits, surveys

The essence of an executive summary is that it is brief. Don't go into detail on the points above. Give the reader the basic facts. If your audience wants to know more about any of these issues they will read the body of the report or any appendices you choose to incorporate. The main part of the report follows this summary and should be laid out in the same sequence. This organization makes it easy for the reader to refer from one section in the summary to the same section in the body. To facilitate referencing, each section of the summary should include a direction to that section in the report. For example: "Detailed information on this topic can be found in Section (name), pages x to y."

Main Report

The key points covered in the executive summary are expanded in the main report. It provides greater detail as well as explanation of certain points. There is usually more *why* information in this part. The report must be clear, concise, and to the point. It must explain both the results and the implications of the situation that was benchmarked.

Rationale. Section by section the report will explain what you did and why you chose to do it that way. You might include the pros and cons relating to your decisions and tell why you decided as you did. An example might be why you chose to benchmark a company outside your industry. Many people think that what happens in their own industry is all that matters. They have not yet become truly aware of the reality of the global market. When we first started our national surveys at the Saratoga Institute in 1986, the majority of the respondents were interested only in data from their industry. The reason was that industry data were what they were being asked for by their executives and boards of directors. About three years later they began to see the light.

Findings. In the findings section you will use terms and metrics with which your audience is familiar and which they apply every day. If you have to use some unfamiliar terms, you might refer the reader to a glossary in the appendix of the report. In terms of familiarity and interest, if return on assets is your company's most important macro measure of corporate performance, be sure that you relate your findings and recommendations to that measure. If market share is the big concern, then focus your study and findings on how you can positively affect your company's position in the market. The objective, as always, is to show the effect on value added for your customer.

This section should also describe the data that were collected and contain the main collection of graphic exhibits. You can display the gap in different ways, expanding on what you showed in the summary. In some cases you might illustrate the relationship of the main value point to related and covarying value points. Sometimes graphics carry only the shortest of titles. I find that expanded labeling either inside or outside the graphic helps clarify the information being displayed. For example, compare Figure 7.1 with Figure 6.1 from Chapter Six. In Figure 7.1 I have shown the intercept rate and annotated it on the right side with the annual rates. Without the three yearly rates — 50 percent, 25 percent, and 20 percent — the viewer has to try to figure out what the rates are. A little extra thought on your part adds a lot to the reader's understanding.

Methods. In the methods section, you will detail the data-gathering methods and any statistical tests you might have applied.

Figure 7.1. Annotated Intercept Rate.

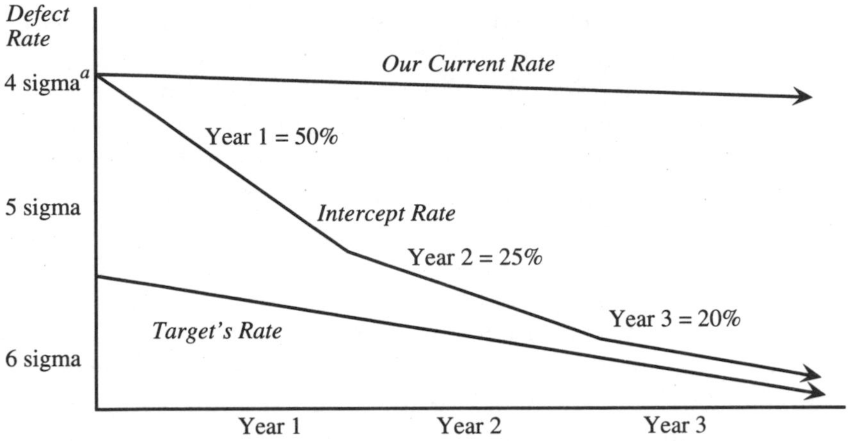

*A sigma is one standard deviation from the mean.

If your organization is dominated by engineers, you know that they love to debate the efficacy of one data-analysis technique versus another. Don't get drawn into that argument but give them enough information so they can see what method you used and why you used it. One of the most useless exercises is to become embroiled in a discussion of process methodology.

The Task. The section on tasks can be broken down into six factors: description of the tasks to be undertaken and completed, resources that will be required, schedule of events and checkpoints, assignment of responsibilities, statement of expected results, and monitoring of progress. This section expands on the recommendations section of your report. You don't want to muddy up the discussion of recommendations by getting involved in a debate over who, what, when, and how they should be done. Make the sale. Then discuss implementation. The goal of your report is to obtain acceptance of your proposals and commitment to act. Afterwards, if you are involved in the change process you can work with the affected group on the details of implementation.

The Human Factor. As always, human beings must make the changes. Two human factors are important to a successful change: committed management and supported, encouraged employees. Management must be sold at the beginning and kept informed along the way. Employees must see by management's actions their commitment is real. If management does not stay involved into the third stage, when change is institutionalized, the change will not hold. Everyone must understand that management is expecting things to be different. The second critical factor is support for the people most affected by the change. Management must see that they have not only resources but also understanding and encouragement. As the new ways of working begin to take hold, the changes should be celebrated. Nothing beats recognition as a reward.

In conclusion, your report is very important. Knowing how to prepare your audience to positively receive your message is the first step. Then, format the report using terms and metrics that you know they will understand and that fit your organization's style. Finally, check in with them as you present the report and when you finish, to see if they understand what you are trying to explain. Connect with them at the value-added level. This critical point is to tell them that you know what is important and that you have data they can use to gain competitive advantage.

Driving Toward the Goal

The purpose of a benchmark report is to accomplish two objectives. One, it should establish the need for change. Two, it should stimulate people to make the change.

The goal of benchmarking is to change an ultimate state, that is, your company's relationship with your customer. The objectives that emerge from a benchmarking project are the path to the ultimate goal. The most important goals of an organization are often expressed in a short list of strategic imperatives. The imperatives, in turn, are driven by the vision and mission of the organization. The vision is your purpose, your raison d'être. It is the most fundamental value that can be expressed.

The vision of the Saratoga Institute, for example, is simple: to be the worldwide source for information and services on staff effectiveness. As part of that goal, we develop both quantitative and qualitative methods and data needed to manage staff departments. This concept keeps us very focused and prevents us from getting into services or functions that are outside our interests and expertise. No one can be all things to all people. We just aim to be the best in one niche. Figure 7.2 maps the path from vision to value.

    To find the goals of your company, check the vision statement that top management has presented. Follow that statement to the strategic imperatives. Today, imperatives tend to revolve around issues such as quality, service, productivity, good citizenship, and respect for employees. Imperatives are the base on which strategies and operating objectives are laid. Each business

Figure 7.2. The Goal Map.

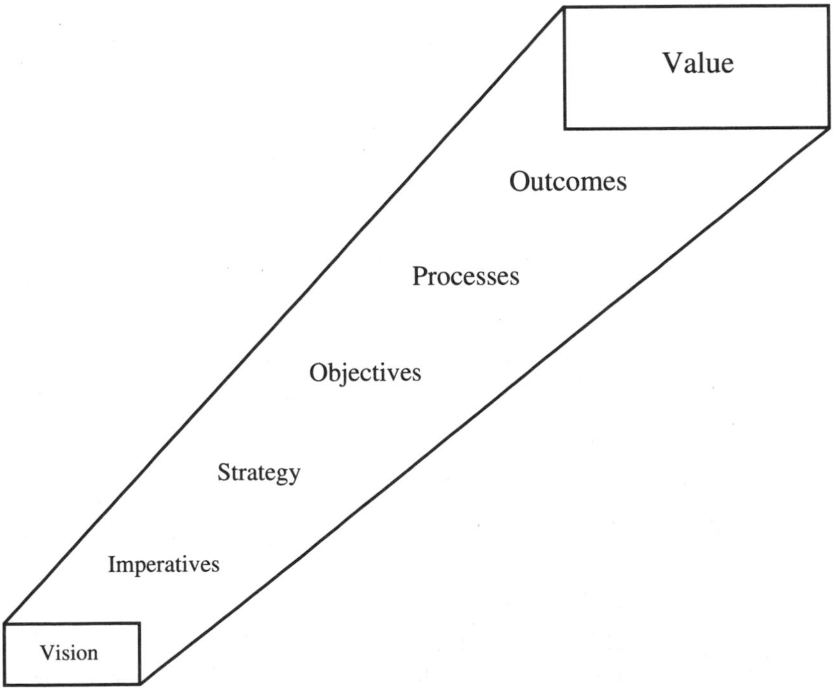

unit develops and pursues a number of quantitative and qualitative objectives each year. Your benchmark findings should provide ideas and comparative data on which decisions can be based to work on achieving certain business objectives. If the objectives are, in fact, a natural progression from the strategic imperatives, you will be able to trace the recommended changes to a value-adding effect on your customers. At Typically Ltd. the trail leads through several staff departments that must improve their processes for the company to regain market share.

Goals and objectives are often based on extrapolating the past into the future. Budgets are the best example of this process. If your budget was five million dollars last year, this year it will probably be within 10 percent of that in either direction. Continual extrapolation can lead an organization off the path because the marketplace is not a continual extension of itself. New technologies, new competitors, new social issues, new political factors are not extensions of the past. They arise, blaze across the sky, and disappear, leaving little trace. What worked yesterday may be totally useless tomorrow. This discontinuity is the nature of the market now and into the foreseeable future.

The critical point is that goals need to be constantly reexamined. Your findings may confirm or refute a long-held belief. If you are benchmarking cost-reduction methods by talking with the best-practice companies, you may have found that cost would continue to be a key success point for those companies. On the other hand, you might have learned that they were shifting to faster service or customization as a driving force. If your company continues to focus on driving costs down it could find itself with the cheapest product but no market. The lesson is that goals should be reviewed for direction, emphasis, and value using the following questions as a guide:

- Are we moving in the right direction in terms of cost, timeliness, quality, product development, customer utility, or other key issues?
- What is the most important issue to focus on now?
- Where should we be allocating resources?
- Where is the greatest value to be found for our customers?

Planning the Change

Change is a much-talked-about and seldom defined process. More has been written about the problems associated with it than about what change actually implies. Kanter provided a high level definition in *The Change Masters* (1983, p. 279): "Change involves the crystallization of new action possibilities (new policies, new behaviors, new patterns, new methodologies, new products, or new market ideas) based on reconceptualized patterns in the organization."

In practice, change has two aspects. One is what has to happen. What tasks must be accomplished to unfreeze the old process, make the change, and stabilize the new process? The other is the human element, to whom it will happen. Who will be affected and how do you help them accept it? In planning, it is useful first to understand the basic dynamics of change.

Stage 1. Unfreezing

In the first stage of the change process you will be creating the motivation to change through your report findings and recommendations. The success of this step will be greatly enhanced if you address sensitively the following concerns of employees:

1. *Concern over expressed lack of confidence in the present system.* Groups have concepts of themselves, their work, and its value. Your data will suggest that the self-concept of the targeted unit is somewhat out-of-date in terms of its value. To tell people that they are not as effective as they thought can be a blow. To soften the impact it is important to prepare the audience before the report is released, particularly if you are going to identify a major performance gap.
2. *Feelings of failure.* Some people take information regarding a need to change as a personal indictment. They may become angry or defensive. In these cases it is particularly important to phrase your recommendations not as fault finding but rather as addressing a common organizational problem that collectively can be analyzed and resolved.

3. *Sense of incompetence and insecurity.* Assuming that there is some willingness among the affected employees to accept information suggesting a need to work differently, they still may perceive the recommendation as a threat and try to block the change. Being asked to adopt new tasks for which they are not trained brings on feelings of incompetence and insecurity. These fears can be handled with assurances that the workers will be given training or other opportunities to learn.

Stage 2. Changing

In the second stage, the change actually begins to take place.

1. *Your report as an information source.* You will have presented the information suggesting change that you have drawn from multiple sources. If your audience is to accept your recommendations, they will have to believe in you and your data. The credibility of your report is the key factor here.
2. *Other sources.* Some people will want to verify your statements by doing some checking of their own. This activity can be useful or destructive, depending on how they go about it. If they tell you they want to check something out on their own, I suggest that you agree, with the stipulation that they first discuss with you what they want to do. The point is to make sure they are checking the same thing you are reporting. If they have missed an important point of your presentation, they may go off and obtain irrelevant data leading them to the wrong conclusions. Then, you have a real problem on your hands.

Stage 3. Refreezing

In the third phase you want to stabilize and integrate the changes.

1. *Getting the changes into the system.* No change will last if it is not institutionalized. Someone must stick with the new pro-

cess until it becomes a natural part of the way of working. Patience and determination are the important traits needed here. Everyone involved must realize that the change will not take place immediately. At the same time, there must be widespread persistence in expecting the change to be made.

2. *Confirming the change.* One important aspect of systems is reward and punishment. People will respond to being rewarded for having changed their behavior and for performing according to the requirements of the new process. Likewise, they will respond to being punished for resisting the new process. It is very important to monitor the change and to recognize people for having accomplished it.

The last phase of the benchmarking project as explained in this chapter is summarized in Exhibit 7.1. This exhibit illustrates the four steps of the action phase as presented for the mythical Sample Company.

Conclusion

Everything starts with and depends on communication. Reporting is your selling opportunity. Your preparation begins with a review of the relationships you have with your audiences. A positive relationship is a prerequisite to persuasion. Then, you learn your audience's interests, values, attitudes, and needs as they relate to the process in question. Finally, you state the benefits or values they and the company will receive if they follow through on your recommendations. This explication is your selling power point: What can we gain by fixing it? and What can we lose if we don't?

Prepare for your presentation. If you have a choice, select the time and place that is most favorable for making your presentation. The environment can enhance or detract from what you have to say. Provide a comfortable space. Avoid presenting to people who are tired or preoccupied. Make it easy for them to see and hear you.

Make your report easy to comprehend. Keep the terminology simple and familiar. Be straightforward. Don't equivocate.

Exhibit 7.1. The Sample Company Staff Benchmarking Project:
Phase IV. Action.

---

1. Preparing to Report

The primary audience for the presentation of this report will be the chief financial officer, the head of sales and marketing, the controller, and the CEO. Others who will read the report are in the accounting, order entry, and sales departments.

We know that the CEO is not deeply interested, so our oral presentation will have to be very concise and to the point. The sales and marketing executive is interested only from the standpoint of how any changes might affect customer relations. The controller and CFO will want to know how the report suggestions might affect cash flow and incidentally work processes.

We will try to schedule a presentation on Monday afternoon in one of the rooms of the conference center rather than in the board room. This location should help to create a positive, problem-solving, collegial atmosphere rather than an "executive review" climate.

2. Structuring the Report

We will first prepare an outline of the full report. From that we will develop the executive summary. In doing the summary we should be able to recognize the key issues and assess how well we have addressed any questions that could come up. In the summary we will discuss the following:

- Project purpose
- Findings
- Recommendations
- Project process and methods

The key point we want to make is the consequences of *not* closing the gap.

The main report will provide more detail on each of these four sections. It will offer a full discussion of the tasks ahead, the resource requirements, a tentative general schedule of events, an outline of responsibilities, realistic expectations, and the monitoring system.

3. Driving Toward the Goal

As we plan and work through this process, we need to keep everyone's thinking and decision making focused on the value goal. We do not want people to get so bogged down in the process that they lose sight of the outcomes we need and why we need them.

We will set the following list of questions in the report and keep referring to them as we move through the project implementation:

a. Are we still moving toward the goal of improving customer satisfaction and improving cash flow?
b. What is the most important issue to focus on at this point? Is importance always defined in terms of measurable value?
c. Where should we be allocating resources at this time?
d. Where is the greatest value to be found for our customers?

Exhibit 7.1. The Sample Company Staff Benchmarking Project:
Phase IV. Action, Cont'd.

---

4. Planning and Leading the Change

Assuming we can convince the company officers to proceed with our recommendations, we have to plan how we will involve the process clerical staff in the changes. We must give them a sense of value and contribution. We do not anticipate any problems within accounting.

We need to communicate with the other stakeholders in sales. As we prepare to make the changes, the sales staff should be informed. They will want to tell their customers that new forms and procedures will be implemented that will make it easier for the customers to process their orders and invoices.

We also want to keep the senior group involved and supportive. This will be done with short weekly or bi-weekly flash progress reports.

Say what you believe without resorting to modifiers and qualifiers. Start by reviewing the purpose of the benchmarking project. Present the findings, followed by your recommendations. Finish with a call for action. Cover process issues last in an oral presentation and address them only if requested. In the process section and in the recommendations describe why you used the method you chose rather than another.

Reexamine the goals of the organization. Are the ones that you started with still important? Have there been any changes that would cause you to suggest redoing the project? Your recommendations must be appropriate to current and foreseeable conditions.

After you have made the sale—presented your findings and recommendations—and if you are involved in the action step, consider both the human and the task side. You depend on people to carry out your plan. Obtain management's commitment and involvement. Keep them involved in the change process until the new process has become part of the system.

First, foremost, and at all times, keep everyone's focus on the value to be added.

8

Managing Large-Scale, Multicompany, and Multinational Benchmarking Projects

Large-scale, multicompany benchmarking projects offer benefits that cannot be obtained from smaller projects. Big projects also require general operating principles that recognize their uniqueness. This chapter describes two large-scale projects, one originating in the United States and one in Australia.

Large benchmarking projects can develop in several ways. One way is for a single company to decide to sponsor the project. Company personnel either make the contacts with benchmarking partners and run the project themselves or they enlist the help of an outside organization, usually a consulting firm, to find the partners and manage the project. In a second method, a number of companies decide they want to benchmark a process together. In this case the expenses are usually shared. As in the first method, they may form a task force and manage the project themselves or they may call on an outside third party. A third method results when a trade or professional association, such as the Edison Electric Institute in Washington, D.C., determines that there would be value in benchmarking something common to all its utility members. The project might be managed by the association staff, with a member task force, or contracted out to a consulting firm. Some-

172

times the expense is covered initially by the association and the results made available later to all members at a small cost. Other cases involve fee-for-service participation. A fourth model rapidly gaining popularity is a network group set up by a third party outside an industry. Examples are the several special-interest networks run by the American Productivity and Quality Center from Houston, Texas, and the HR Benchmark Network managed by the Saratoga Institute out of Saratoga, California. These programs offer fee-based memberships and take on benchmarking projects desired by the members. Still another technique is for an outsider such as a consulting firm to propose to a group of companies that they participate in a project. In this case, all participating companies share the expense or pay a fee to take part.

Controlling the Process

No matter the source, a multicompany or multinational project is complex to manage because of the many participants. If the topic were a single process, such as order entry or service dispatching, managing would be a bit less difficult. However, when several people are involved they often bring with them a wide range of interests. Their position is usually that, considering the effort they must expend, they may as well broaden the investigation. This attitude can lead to problems as the list of processes grows. Therefore, some controls need to be built in. One project cannot solve all problems.

Whether the process is run by the sponsor or by a consultant, it must be kept under control. If it opens up too much, a great deal of effort will be expended by everyone involved to address all the issues placed on the agenda. For every topic that is added to the investigation, more than one extra question will have to be developed, explored, and reported on. For every question, unspoken expectations develop. In the end, the chances are better than fifty-fifty that some participants will be disappointed.

General Issues and Principles

The rules of procedure for large-scale, multicompany benchmarking are similar to those for a small project; there are just more players to be considered. Each has a role and a set of responsibilities. As you add people to the process, the considerations and responsibilities multiply. Exhibit 8.1 is an outline of responsibilities and the participants who must execute them that are generic to all large-scale projects. They will vary only with a project's idiosyncrasies.

The issues, roles, and responsibilities will vary somewhat depending on who sponsors the project. If it is a typical project with one company sponsoring it, the sponsor roles are clearer. If several companies are the de facto sponsors, then the sponsors' activities may be divided among the companies or a task force may drive the project, with the labor apportioned among the various players. If no consultant is involved, those duties will also have to be assumed by the sponsors. The outline in Exhibit 8.1 assumes one sponsor with a consultant managing the project under the direction of the sponsor. The duties can be allocated between the sponsor and the consultant as the sponsor wishes.

This model was used in two projects. One covered the entire range of one of the major functions of a staff department. It was sponsored by an American company and managed by a consultant. The other originated in Australia and was managed by an Australian consultant for two Australian companies. It covered a variety of topics related to organizational effectiveness and human resources. Both projects are described here; the more typical one, the U.S.–based project, is discussed first.

Project I: U.S. Sponsor

The U.S. project was sponsored by an electronic company and enlisted almost three dozen benchmarking partners representing half a dozen industries spread across the country. It began in the fall of 1991. The Saratoga Institute (SI) was contacted by the sponsor and a meeting was arranged to look at the project. After discussion of the project objectives, an agreement was reached that SI would be retained to manage the project, proceeding through the following steps:

Exhibit 8.1. Outline of Roles and Responsibilities in Large Projects.

Players

Sponsor: Company that initiated and is driving the project
Consultant: Hired by the sponsor to direct the project
Partners: Companies that will participate in the project

Phase A

Roles

Sponsor: To set initial scope of the project
Consultant: To provide expertise and manage the project to meet sponsor's needs
Partners: To contribute ideas (possibly) and data to the project

Duties

Sponsor: Work with consultant on issues to be benchmarked
Identify desirable partners, specifically or in general
Determine criteria for partnership
Place boundaries on sources for partners
Agree on potential partner contact method

Consultant: Clarify expectations of sponsor regarding process and results
Possibly research the state-of-the-art on the topic
Develop questions with sponsor
Design questionnaire and data collection forms
Discuss round table logistics and clarify roles
Develop time schedule with sponsor
Enlist partners
Mail or have sponsor mail questionnaire with cover letter
Call partners to clarify and probe
Summarize partner responses and feedback for verification
Assemble data from all partners
Prepare preliminary report

Partners: Commit resources to project
Develop data
Share data

Phase B

Duties:

Sponsor: Schedule and host round table
Mail out final report with thank-you letter

Consultant: Facilitate round table
Collect and analyze results
Prepare final report
Make presentation to sponsor with recommendations

Partners: Participate in round table

---

1. Defining the scope of the inquiry and designing a questionnaire
2. Recruiting benchmarking partners
3. Mailing the questionnaire with a schedule and agenda
4. Making follow-up phone calls
5. Writing a preliminary report
6. Coordinating a two-day round table meeting of participants
7. Writing a final report

Because the participating companies were in thirty-four locations spread across the United States, the sponsoring organization did not feel that site visits were necessary or feasible from the standpoint of time and cost. On-site observations would not have added much data that could not be obtained through a questionnaire and follow-up telephone interviews. The expense of travel would have doubled the final cost of the benchmarking effort. The project took over six months from the time the initial scope of the investigation was determined until the final report was mailed.

Setting the Scope

The sponsoring company set the scope of the project in terms of the areas that were to be benchmarked. Initially an internal task force was assembled and a preliminary list of questions was developed. At this point it became clear that the project had already grown beyond its original intent and that the amount of work involved would be impossible for the staff to carry out, given their ongoing responsibilities. The decision was made to contact a consultant to provide guidance and probably to manage the project. Consultants are not always necessary but they do bring certain advantages. In a multicompany project, the consultant can contribute two important qualities: impartiality and confidentiality. The consultant can also dedicate total resources to a project while in-house staff usually have other responsibilities also. But the consultant should never take over the project because then there will be no inside ownership of the results.

At the first meeting the consultant reviewed the questionnaire and recommended that it be shortened. He did not believe that partners would engage in a project requiring the amount of detail demanded by the questionnaire in its original form. In addition, the sponsor's team was told that their company would also have to gather data on each item to share. Subsequently, they reduced the questions to a manageable number. With guidance from the consultant, the internal project team designed the final questionnaire. It consisted of a combination of check-offs, ratings, and open-ended descriptions. Questionnaires should be kept as short as possible. If the project is successful, additional data can be sought in a subsequent phase.

The sponsoring company's team decided that they wanted to host a two-day round table after the data were obtained. Attendance of partners would be optional. The consultant agreed that this was an effective vehicle for getting deep into the data and for sharing experiences that cannot be easily captured on a questionnaire. A tentative date and agenda for the meeting were set. The round table turned out to be the most valuable aspect of the project.

Selecting Partners

A list of potential benchmark partners was drawn up jointly by the sponsor's team and the consultant. The selection pool included key companies from the sponsor's industry, companies believed to be best-in-class performers in the topic function regardless of industry, and companies experiencing some of the same operating problems as the sponsor. Chapter Four listed possible sources for locating benchmarking partners, some of which were utilized. The benefit of having industry partners is that you learn what the industry trends are. The downside is that you seldom find breakthrough ideas inside your own industry. History show that most innovations do not come from large, old-line companies. The upstarts who have one breakthrough product and who are fighting for their lives often are the best sources for the most original ideas.

Typically, partnership criteria cover such categories as industry, company size, geographic region, and growth rate.

Although excellent performance can be found in companies of all types, sometimes it is not transferable. This is especially true of companies that are vastly different in size. The volume, scope, or need for sophisticated data handling in one company may not apply in another.

The consultant helped the internal team draft a letter of invitation describing the project, to be written, signed, and mailed by the sponsor. The consultant developed a data collection form for the interviewers' use and prepared a spreadsheet to record and compute the data that would be obtained. The letter of invitation was mailed. One week after the letters were received by the companies invited to participate, the consultant called each of them to obtain answers to two questions: Were they interested in participating and did they have the capability to obtain the data needed to participate? Sometimes individuals desire to share data but their company will not allow it, fearing that they are giving away a competitive advantage. This is true not only in production and sales but also in some staff situations. From an original list of fifty-six companies a final set of thirty-four decided to participate. This was nearly double the number the sponsor had anticipated.

Data Collection

The consultant then mailed the questionnaire to the partners. Approximately two weeks later, his staff began their calls to the partners. Data were collected, written up, and verified with the participants. Then the quantitative data were put into the spreadsheet and the narrative was transcribed into a text file. The data were reviewed and several callbacks were made for final clarification. Even after data have been verified, it is sometimes difficult to perceive anomalies until all the data are in and the ranges can be seen.

Protocols on data collection were outlined in Chapter Five. In accordance with these, consideration was given to the partners' time and sensitivities. In this step, preparing partners for the call so that it comes at a convenient time for them is critical to obtaining complete data. Keeping the interview focused is also important. Start with the most general question and move

to the most specific. Throughout the process, honesty and frank-
ness are critical. Once trust is lost, the game is over. Be sure
to thank people for their time and willingness to share; without
them you would not have a project. Remember that planning,
sensitivity, and focus are the hallmarks of effective data collection. These protocols were all followed in the project described
here.

Preliminary Report

After final checking, a preliminary report was prepared and
mailed to all those who chose to participate in the round table.
It presented the summary quantitative data along with the narrative. Individual company responses were not identified, although some of the comments were transcribed verbatim in the
discussion section. Eighteen of the thirty-four companies were
able to travel to the meeting. The preliminary report was not
mailed to the others. The project team believed that for them
to receive two reports would be confusing. They would later
be given the preliminary results as part of the final report.

Round Table Meeting

The sponsoring company chose to handle the logistics of the
round table since they were paying the bill. The sponsor and
the consultant worked out the agenda and reciprocal roles. The
format consisted of a series of general meetings for an exchange
of views, followed by sessions with smaller groups for special
topic discussions. The small groups then reported in the general
meeting. The consultant led the plenary session and shared facili-
tation of the small groups with sponsor personnel. Recorders
from the sponsor's and the consultant's organizations were assigned to each session so that all comments could be captured
for later incorporation into the final report.

Final Report

The consultant was given all the data from the round table meetings and spent the next two weeks preparing a final report. This

study did not include longitudinal data, so it was difficult to show relationships between given activities and apparently related results. Some conclusions were drawn and, where possible, recommendations were made. The final report was mailed by the sponsor with a thank-you letter to all partners.

To analyze data productively you need to go beyond simply regurgitating it. You need to look for patterns and relationships. You need to answer the question, why does someone do it this way? Careful study will lead you to connections that are the causal or correlational factors you seek. You will see that one item increases, another moves either with it or in the opposite direction. Reports that disclose these relationships can be extremely helpful in determining where to put your resources.

Presentation

On completion of the written report, an oral report was prepared for the sponsor's benchmarking team. All the project staff acknowledged that they had gained something of value. In the beginning there was some disappointment that evidence was not as conclusive as the team members had hoped it would be. This was attributable to the scope of the investigation as well as to the constraints that were put on it in terms of time and budget. Nevertheless, after taking time to digest the report and talking at length with the consultant about the project results, the team developed a new appreciation for what they had achieved. All agreed that they had produced useful information and that they had learned a great deal about benchmarking. In the end, they were ready to take on another benchmarking project.

Reflections

This project was a valuable learning experience for the sponsor's personnel. Beyond benchmarking, they learned much about handling data. The sponsor learned to have realistic expectations regarding what future projects could produce as well as the amount of resources required to carry out such a venture. Because of budget limitations, some of the steps recommended by the consultant could not be undertaken. This constraint adversely affected the depth of detail desired by the sponsor. To end on a positive note, however, the sponsor's team suggested several methodologies for discussing the data at the round table; these suggestions added greatly to the participants' understanding and assimilation of the mass of data produced in the project.

Project II: Australian Sponsors

The Australian project was sponsored by National Australia Bank and Comalco Minerals and Alumina. They had been involved in the Australian version of the Society for Human Resource Management (SHRM) and Saratoga Institute Human Resource Effectiveness (HRE) program and they wanted to know more about how some of the American companies had achieved their results. The sponsors developed their needs by working with HRM Consulting of Brisbane, the Australian manager of the HRE program. The Saratoga Institute served as the U.S. consultant on the project.

Scope

The sponsors were interested in strategies and processes across five broad categories:

Organizational effectiveness

- Organizational development
- Communications

Human resource (HR) management effectiveness

- Strategic HR management
- Continuous HR improvement

Practices and processes to decrease absence and turnover

- Mergers and acquisitions
- Work and family

Training and development effectiveness

- Training
- Management development

Succession planning and staffing effectiveness

- Performance appraisal
- Recruitment and selection
- Succession and career planning
- Temporary staffing

Partner Selection

Two criteria were used to select companies for what came to be called the International HR Best Practices Report. Companies had to satisfy at least one of the following criteria to be included as a benchmarking partner: (1) be in the top 10 percent on key measures in the U.S. Human Resources Effectiveness Report published by SHRM/Saratoga Institute (1971), or (2) have a reputation for eminence in human resources management. Based on these criteria, the following companies were selected by the sponsors:

Amdahl	Intel
Bank One	MCI Communications
Baxter	Mellon Bank
Colgate	Memorial Sloan-Kettering
Connecticut Mutual Life	Cancer Center
Federal Express	Motorola
First Tennessee Bank	Pacific Gas and Electric
GMAC Mortgage	Rohm and Haas
	Whirlpool

Data Collection

The Australian consultant prepared and mailed a set of questions to the benchmark companies after they had been contacted by phone. Each company was given time to study the questions.

A short follow-up call was made and site visits were scheduled. In most cases, an interviewer from the sponsoring companies and one from HRM Consulting took part in the site visits, which were done in June and July 1992.

For gathering data, the project team had developed twelve subtopics under the five general strategy and practice areas. Each company was queried on two or three of the twelve. Each was asked about particular topics on the basis of their performance as presented in the HRE Report or because they had an excellent reputation on those topics, or both. A structured questionnaire was used for the queries (see Exhibit 8.2). The items on the questionnaire are only starter questions; much follow-up questioning was carried out.

In addition to the data collected during the interviews, the participating companies provided information about their organizations. The material ranged from annual reports to detailed descriptions of their strategies and practices.

Report

HRM Consulting produced a comprehensive report for all participants in December 1992. It displayed the various strategies and practices with rationales for each. It described not only what the best practice companies were doing but why. One example came from a company studied for its team building and use of surveys in the organizational development area. The key points were outlined as follows: (1) Teamwork is important enough to be addressed specifically in the company's mission statement, and (2) An important element of teamwork is the use of survey feedback to encourage horizontal and vertical communication. Three types of surveys are used:

- From team members on each other
- From team members on the team as a whole
- From team members on the leader

The report provided more detail and also discussed how the other five partners used surveys in pursuit of organizational

Exhibit 8.2. Format for Benchmarking Interview.

---

1. Could you explain to me how Human Resources (HR) fits into the organization's structure?

   - *Get copy of the organization chart if possible.*
   - *Is HR part of the organization's senior structure?*

2. Thinking back over the last twelve months or so, what are some of the major strategies that the organization has undertaken?

   How did HR find out about these strategies? Did HR have a role in their formation or were they told later? If they had a role, what was it?

3. Thinking about HR as a whole in your organization, what are some of the areas that your organization handles better than most other organizations?

   Probes (tick for later follow-up):

   _____ Succession planning
   _____ Training and development
   _____ Handling plateaued workers
   _____ Selecting senior management
   _____ Handling poor performers
   _____ Handling high-potential people
   _____ Managing acquisitions
   _____ Quality HR management and reporting HR function
   _____ Career/family balance and mobility
   _____ Staff consultation/communication strategies

4. (a) Could you tell us more about this area? (ticked above)

   - *Get as concrete information as possible.*
   - *Get physical material.*

   (b) This sounds like an excellent program. Do you have any measures that have helped you form the opinion that this is a good program?

   - *Get as much detail on the measurement process as possible. Was it reactive? a pre- or post-measure? dollar converted?*

   By the end of question 4, cover the following:

   - Why did you do the program/intervention and so on?
   - How have you done it?
   - What are the actual steps?
   - Is there anything you would do differently now? Why?
   - Can the results of the intervention be or have they been converted into a dollar value or some other impact measure?

Exhibit 8.2. Format for Benchmarking Interview, Cont'd.

---

5. *Repeat 4 above for ticked but not yet converted areas.*

   • *If possible, confirm above information on ticked areas with informal probes to other organization members, such as, "I heard x was really good. . . ."*

6. (a) How would you describe the culture of the organization?

   Probes: Do they have slogans, heroes, stories? If so, what are they?

   (b) How big a part did your culture play in the success of the program/ intervention? If it was a big part, how do you maintain and encourage this aspect of your culture?

   If it was a hindrance, how did you overcome it and maintain the change?

7. There is a lot of talk about adding value (and your programs obviously are), but what do you do to demonstrate your success (impacts/value adding) to your (hard-nosed, diffident) manager?

8. (a) What do you see as some of the emerging issues for your organization?

   (b) What are some of the HR responses to these emerging issues that you are thinking of using or that you hear other people or companies are using?

   Get names of other individuals or companies for later contact if they seem relevant.

---

improvement. Collectively, the partners learned through the report how the best partners were handling each of the twelve areas. From this information they could draw lessons and adapt whatever seemed to fit their culture. The sponsors were also interviewed about those areas in which they felt they had an excellent practice. Their data were incorporated into the report.

Reflections

An international study adds extra elements such as distance and cultural differences to data collection and interpretation. These factors — particularly the cultural differences — can cause some difficulty in generalizing the learning. Nevertheless, most industrialized nations show surprising similarity in their staff processes. The differences usually occur in the laws, the underlying values, and the emphasis given to one factor versus another. Because there has been so much contact across borders among the larger multinational companies, a good bit of homogenization has already taken place. So, although customs, laws, and regulations may be different among partners, useful lessons can be learned from international benchmarking.

Conclusion

Broad-scale projects can be extremely powerful. However, they generate special problems that should be anticipated. One is the practical problem of assimilating a mass of data. To verify that a practice is truly effective, you must be able to draw correlations between activities and quantifiable results. While it is not necessary to attempt proof at a statistical level, it is desirable to be able to show convincing face-value data suggesting the connection. Establishing this link takes a great deal of analysis, which is not always appreciated by the client. In most cases, it is better to take a smaller bite and be able to savor the texture and flavor thoroughly than to wolf down a big piece and suffer indigestion.

Multicompany projects also raise expectations that are not always expressed up front by the partners. Later, when they do not find what they are looking for, they are disappointed. It is important to draw out as many expectations as possible in the beginning to avoid later discontent. Having the expected outcome formulated clearly also helps partners focus when answering or asking questions. If possible, it is very useful to have the partners state what they believe the data might do for them — that is, what is the perceived value of having the benchmark information? When this end result is clear to the partner, the sponsor, and the consultant, then conscious effort can be made to ensure that the necessary data are generated. Without this direction, everyone is working in the dark and someone is bound to be frustrated. Like every other activity, a successful benchmarking project is driven by preparation, focused energy, insight, and an understanding of the values involved.

9

A National Benchmarking Project:
Uncovering the True Source
of Best Practices

*A great deal of discussion and work related to best prac-
tices has taken place in recent years. In the business
world, we often take off running without clearly defining our destination or verifying the maps we are using.
The following study was an attempt by the Saratoga
Institute to identify best practices starting from a quantitative performance base and applying a set of clear,
objective decision-making rules. What we learned shed
new light on so-called best practices.*

This chapter describes a benchmarking study carried out from the fall of 1991 through the summer of 1992 to
examine excellence in relations with employees. In August 1992,
the Saratoga Institute published a report detailing general findings and specific case examples of what were determined to be
best practices. The report tested the methodology and provided
the initial results for what was to become the Best in America
program, launched by SI to recognize exceptional performance
in productivity, process management, and service within HR
departments. The first recognition came in the form of the Best
Practice Report in 1992.

This project is another example of a multicompany benchmarking effort. It was originally undertaken to answer the question continually asked of the SI staff: "Who is doing the best
at (fill in the blank)." Before we could launch the study we had
to decide on a definition of the term *best*.

Defining *Best*

The word *best* is a superlative in the English language. A thesaurus offers a long list of synonyms including the following:

superior	superlative	largest
optimal	first-rate	superb
top	preeminent	unsurpassed

Clearly, the word is meant to express something exceptional. When it is applied to a person, a thing, an action, or a condition, it literally means that this case is better than all others of its type. When *best* is applied to a business practice, it supposedly refers to one that represents the ideal.

Business people like to be able to identify something as best so that they can copy it or model their behavior after it. However, this is where they run into problems. Although the idea of *best* implies a universality, in operation, it is very difficult to prove that there is one best way of doing something. The mismatch occurs because the judgment of *best* implies a set of fixed criteria. In business, nothing is fixed. What is good for one company is not necessarily good for another. This variation reflects the effect of performance drivers in different companies. Only after we have agreed on the criteria can we begin to search for the best of anything. Are we going to define *best* according to cost, time, quality, or other measurable criteria? Without this agreement we are looking for an invisible example. I am not attempting to beg the question here but rather to frame it in a practical context.

When we set out to benchmark a best practice, we need to define what *best* means in our situation. Would we say that the best is synonymous with the cheapest or the most expensive? Is it something that is accomplished in the shortest period of time or does time matter? Should it have the fewest defects or can faster response make up for a minor error or two? Is the outcome to be the best for the employees, management, shareholders, or community? The answer is, of course, "It depends." It depends on what is most important to us.

Setting Criteria

Periodically, publications trumpet the exploits of an individual or group and proclaim them as "best something." Yet, when we investigate the criteria on which the judgment was made we often find flaws. Frequently there was no objective basis for the designation of *best*. In short, it was a popularity contest. Often the sampled population was extremely small and the data not generalizable. I'm not advocating that we need one thousand companies analyzed to the third decimal point. I am suggesting that you should beware of what you read.

To be labeled *best,* the object must satisfy the highest objective standards across as many dimensions as possible. In businesses, these typically include costs, time, quantity, quality, and human reactions. In operation, the ideal state is seldom if ever realized. A process or practice that yields exceptional results in one setting may not be effective in another. In fact, it may be counterproductive. The wholesale adoption of one organization's practice may not work for another organization. In almost all cases some modification is necessary. All we can really say at the end of a benchmarking project is that this practice, process, or strategy is the best that we looked at among all that we benchmarked, having applied certain criteria to demonstrate clearly that we would have objective, measurable results to compare. If we have those data, we can call what we examined a "best practice."

The criteria applied in the study described in this chapter were drawn from the measures reported in the 1991 edition of the *Human Resources Effectiveness Report* (HRER). The HRER is a study of human resource related activities and outcomes published annually since 1986 by SI and sponsored by the Society for Human Resource Management (SHRM). In 1991, data had been obtained on nearly six hundred companies. The report provides quantitative data on hiring, pay and benefits, training, turnover, and absenteeism. Approximately thirty cost, time, and quantity factors are reported.

As a related issue, given that these companies demonstrated excellence in managing some aspects of their relations with employees, could we find a connection between those practices and exceptional operating and financial performance? At the outset we thought the findings would be interesting. No matter what they turned out to be, we knew we could not demonstrate a linear connection between one or two practices and total corporate performance. Nevertheless, we believed the results would provide some data that might be studied each year for possible long-term correlations.

The Benchmarks

Our study of best performance went through three stages: (1) defining best performance, (2) contacting qualifying organizations, and (3) distributing a questionnaire in preparation for telephone interviews. In the first stage, determining where to set criteria for best performance, we decided to extract the companies that made up the best twenty-fifth percentile of each of the factors measured. We established this as an initial standard of exceptional performance. The HRER factors on which performance was reported are listed in Exhibit 9.1. These indicators were originally developed in 1984 through a task force formed by the Saratoga Institute under the sponsorship of the American Society for Personnel Administration (the original name of the Society for Human Resource Management). They are updated each year in the HRER report.

This first cut yielded 110 companies. Some of the companies qualified in several of the measures listed in Exhibit 9.1. Some qualified in only one. No one qualified in all areas. By using quantitative data that had a six-year record of verification and validity, we were assured of a solid base for beginning the selection process. These metrics are the benchmarks of exceptional performance as judged against six hundred companies in twenty industries.

In the second stage, the qualifying organizations were contacted initially by letter notifying them that they had passed the first level of qualification as a best-practice operation. A follow-up phone call was made to each of the 110 organizations. They were asked, in general, how they could account for their exceptional results. We received three types of responses.

Exhibit 9.1. SHRM/Saratoga Institute
National Standard Human Resource Measures.

Revenue/employee	Compensation/revenue
Operating expense/employee	Compensation/operating expense
Human resource expense/operating expense	Benefit cost/revenue
Human resource headcount/employees	Benefit cost/operating expense
Human resource expense/employees	Benefit cost/compensation
Workers Compensation claims/employees	Retiree benefit costs/benefit costs
Workers Compensation costs	Retiree benefit costs/retiree
Absentee percentage	Accession (hire) percentage
Turnover percentage	Cost per hire
Voluntary turnover percentage	Time to fill requisitions
Involuntary turnover percentage	Time to fill jobs
Voluntary turnover by length of service	Offer-to-acceptance ratio
Training cost	Training hours
Trainee hours	

One group of companies were unaware that they had done a superior job. They could not identify any specific action that might have caused the outcomes. These were what is sometimes called the "unconscious competent." Unfortunately, as they did not have a knowledgeable grasp of their own operation, they could not describe their processes well enough for us to continue the investigation. It appeared likely that their superior results were more a matter of uncontrolled, fortuitous circumstances than planned actions. In a few cases, the companies did not want to share their data publicly.

A second group of companies admitted that they had been lucky. They could not point to any specific action that might have caused their results to reach this level. Therefore, they could not be documented as a best-practice operation. After talking with the first and second groups we eliminated nearly eighty companies from the study.

The third group acknowledged that they had developed a conscious strategy by which they ran their operations. As a result of these deliberate efforts they were able to improve their operation and sustain it at high levels. This group constituted the thirty-three finalists.

Benchmarking the Practices

In the third stage, each of the finalist companies was mailed a questionnaire that would be the basis for another phone interview. They were asked to consider what they did, how they did it, and who was involved. The initial "issue" questions are listed in Exhibit 9.2. Questions three through seven give us the basic information on what the processes are, how they are run, and why they were designed that way. From the responses to these questions, secondary- and tertiary-level questions would be posed during the interview. After giving respondents two weeks to recollect how they had achieved their results, they were interviewed by telephone again. In the course of these interviews another eleven companies were eliminated for one or another reason. This left the final best practice population at

Exhibit 9.2. Best Practice Benchmark Questions.

---

1. Is this your first year participating in the HRER? If not, were this year's results much better than those of previous years with regard to the category or categories in which you performed exceptionally well?
2. Describe, in general, what happened in the past year that helped you to achieve your exceptionally good results.
3. When did the changes take place, and how long did they take to implement?
4. How were these changes different from those of previous years?
5. Why did you make these changes? Were they initiated by something that occurred inside or outside the company?
6. Where did you get the idea or model you used? Did it occur within headquarters, or was it a field division?
7. Who else was involved in the effort? Was senior management involved before, during, or after?
8. As a result of your work, have you noticed a difference within the HR department and/or within the company in terms of productivity or quality? Have you noticed a difference on a human level?
9. Did you present this material to top management? What was their reaction?
10. Can we use your name and the name of your company in SI's annual Best Practices Report?

---

twenty-two. These companies represented the best 4 percent of the original *Human Resources Effectiveness Report* population of nearly six hundred companies.

The Best Practices Group Profile

The twenty-two companies that make up the best practices group represent the following industries: chemicals, consumer products, finance, general manufacturing, health care, insurance, pharmaceuticals, semiconductors, telecommunications, and transportation. They range in size from a midwestern insurance company with about two hundred employees to an East Coast telecommunications company employing about twenty-five thousand. The distribution by size is as follows:

Number of Employees	Number of Companies
1–500	2
501–1000	2
1,001–2,000	3
2,001–5,000	4
5,001–10,000	5
10,001–20,000	4
over 20,000	2

Several of the companies are relatively young, fast-growing firms. Others have been in business for more than one hundred years.

These demographics indicate that no single industry has a monopoly on good human resource management practices. Likewise, best practices are not the exclusive province of large companies or a function of a large human-resource staff. In fact, one of the best of the best is a company with fewer than five hundred employees. The leaders are those companies that exhibit certain positive managerial philosophies, such as commitment, good communications, focus on customers, conscious planning for excellence, and others discussed later in the chapter.

General Findings

The focus of the interviews was on the strategies and practices that drove the twenty-two companies' results. In most instances we discovered that the current results were simply the latest incremental improvements from a program or plan that had been in place for at least two or three years. In several cases, these outcomes and impacts were living examples of continuous-improvement strategies that were yielding the outcomes expected.

The drivers of the outcomes were definitely the human resources staffs. Very seldom had the impetus for change been provided by senior management. This finding confirmed what we have witnessed over the years. The leading departments in all functions do not wait for permission to do something, nor are they responding to orders. In almost all instances they are ahead of their customers and their market. Their behavior is an operational definition of proactivity.

Improvements were not necessarily universal throughout a company. That is, in large corporations we found some units that were far superior to others. Within human resource departments, we found some functions that were achieving much better results than others. This observation further supported our earlier findings, which were described in *Human Value Management* (Fitz-enz, 1991). Exceptional results are the product of people who are driven to excel. In short, performance is a human issue, and exceptional performance cannot be dictated. It results when skilled people are determined to achieve excellence.

The high achievers we interviewed had established personal relationships with peers, internal customers, and senior executives, who became important elements in the drive to fulfill the achievers' vision. High achievers are persuasive people who are able to present a business case for what they are recommending. They described for us how they showed the problem or opportunity, the expected return on investment, and a factor of equal impact: the downside of not doing what was being suggested. Our experience shows that people react more quickly to an acknowledged problem than to a predicted value. We believe that some people are driven more by the fear of failure than they are by the prospect of success.

Application and Implementation of the Data

Keep in mind that this is not a typical benchmarking project as described in Chapters Four through Seven. This project is offered as one more example of the range of work that benchmarking can cover. As such, the utilization of the data is unique to this type of project.

The data elicited by the questions in Exhibit 9.2 are, by definition, correlated with specific best employee-related performance measures. First, we looked for best metrics. Then, we backed into the processes that drove those results. Anyone reading SI's Best Practices Report on one of the twenty-two final companies knows that the company described was among the top 4 percent of six hundred companies in that function. I don't know of any other published study that has identified the best company on a given activity drawing on such a large number of firms.

In seeking possible connections to corporate productivity and financial results, we checked two factors: revenue growth rate and profitability.

Revenue

The HRER provides data on annual revenue growth. It defines three levels: low is 5 percent or less year-to-year growth; medium is 6 percent to 20 percent; high is more than 20 percent growth.

Profitability

Two factors were used in the HRER to determine profitability: revenue per employee and operating expense per employee. By subtracting the expense-from-revenue figure we were left with before-tax income per employee. Armed with these data points for the twenty-two finalists we uncovered the profiles shown in Table 9.1.

Table 9.1. Revenue and Profitability Profiles
for the Twenty-Two Companies.

Revenue Growth Rate		
Twenty-Two Companies		*Levels*
4	=	High
11	=	Medium
7	=	Low
Profitability		
Twenty-Two Companies		*Industry Standing*
9	=	Above industry mean
13	=	Below industry mean

As you can see in Table 9.1, there is no clear pattern to the results, and this is no surprise. We did not expect to see a correlation between a small number of excellent employee-related outcomes and total corporate profitability. If any staff function possessed such power, it would have become evident long ago. The profile does tell us that exceptional performance can take place under any circumstances. In this case, one or more human resources functions were performed at a very high level in seven companies that were experiencing low growth and thirteen that were less profitable than average. In short, ideal conditions are not prerequisite for effective staff performance.

Gap Analysis

In order to do a gap analysis, the reader who wishes to bench-mark his or her company can obtain a copy of the HRER and compare his or her company's data to the twenty-fifth percentile in the report. This comparison will identify the gap. The best practices that are at least partly responsible for the gap have been detailed in the report. The question of how to introduce changes in the readers' companies that will help them close the gap is beyond the scope of SI's Best Practice Report (BPR), or any report for that matter. The BPR provides benchmark metrics, values, and practices and says to the reader, adapt what you can. This is true in any benchmarking project. In the end, each of us has to figure out what to do with the data from a benchmarking exercise.

Insight: The Hidden Source of Best Practices

As we prepared the data for our 1992 Best Practices Report I slowly realized what the basic lesson of this project was. We took testimony from companies on the same function and found that their approaches were diametrically opposed, yet they had both achieved exceptional results. At first, I thought this outcome was merely a manifestation of *best* as an idiosyncratic concept; it is never exactly the same for different situations. However, the more I studied the data, the more I came to realize the secret of *best:*

> **A best practice is not defined by the way a process is structured or carried out. It is a function of a set of background values, strategies, and interactions. These are the constants. These are the driving forces. These are what make organizations the *best*.**

As I went back and forth over the data while writing the report, a pattern gradually emerged of common factors observable in all twenty-two best practice companies. These are the foundation of best practices.

About nine practices were exhibited by nearly every company in the best practice group. I say "about" nine, because additional insights continue to develop the more we talk with and about the people in the twenty-two companies involved in the project. Subsequent editions of the BPR may yield still more generalizable factors. We have seen several of the current factors in other studies of staff management. Conversely, we have seldom found failure among groups who exhibited and were guided by these values, traits, and strategies. Exhibit 9.3 is an outline of the nine factors, which are discussed below. They are listed in alphabetical order since we have not determined at this point the relative power of each.

Exhibit 9.3. Values, Strategies,
and Traits of Best Practice Companies.

Commitment. Having strong determination to stay the course
Communications. Paying exceptional attention to employee communications
Culture consciousness. Fitting systems and programs into the culture
Customer focused. Being proactively attentive to customer needs
Interdependence. Recognizing the influence of one function's work on others
Never satisfied. Being deeply committed to the continuous improvement ethic
Relationships. Building alliances to gain support and complete the work
Risk-taking. Not always asking or obtaining permission
Strategy and planning. Doing what management books prescribe

Commitment

In the United States, we lament top management's lack of long-term commitment to improvement programs. We cite the success of the Japanese as an example of the benefit of commitment to an ideal. The business press reports case after case of quality projects that failed because top management withdrew from active participation soon after launching the program. The Best Practice companies are showcases of commitment to a vision of constant improvement.

One problem with commitment to programs is that a slavish focus on methodology carries within it the seeds of obsolescence. As market conditions change the methods may no longer work as well. One of two things can happen. The first is a total devotion to the methods and systems in which everyone has personally invested so much. Some refuse to give up even when it is obvious that the methods are no longer effective. The second reaction is to make a marked shift away from the old, no longer useful method to something new that should be more appropriate to today's problems. The change brings with it disruption, confusion, and inefficiency.

The Best Practice companies show us a better way. Their commitment is to a vision of what they are and the role they play. The ideal can be to achieve world-class quality, to be the best in customer service, to have the highest productivity, to empower employees, or some other goal. Whatever the vision is, it is not bound by methodology. An internal staff group may seek to position itself as a value-adding business partner of the line functions. In this case, their plans, programs, and processes are designed to support that vision. Just as form follows function, methodology follows commitment. In the case of these companies, the payoff for commitment is obvious. The vision was appropriate and their actions are flexible and unrelenting. The result is excellence.

Communications

The Best Practice companies carry employee communication well beyond the norm. They go to great lengths to communicate with the rank and file. Perhaps more important, they put great effort into stimulating and supporting upward communications. They do not seem to fear what they might learn because they have experimented with unusual, sometimes high-risk methods of obtaining feedback from employees.

One example of an unusual communication came from a company that conducts tests of employee knowledge of their benefits. The objective is to enhance the employees' knowledge so they will use the benefits more cost effectively. Employees are given short quizzes regarding details of the benefits. Their scores are not entered into their personal records. The individual responses are studied and instances of lack of knowledge are identified. Then, an on-the-spot response can be made. Later, some communiqué can be designed to cover areas of employee confusion.

Although we found ingenious methods for promoting two-way communications, the secret is not in the media. The key is the imperative to communicate. The successful companies make communications a daily, primary duty of the total staff. In other words, communications is not a task but a way of life.

Culture Consciousness

Some corporate cultures that worked well in the first decades after World War II are now sicknesses that are plaguing American business. Despite the highlight stories carried in the business literature, there are many companies whose cultures have gradually devolved from positive to negative forces over the past two decades. The human resources department often has a central role in supporting some aspects of the culture as well as helping it change where necessary.

I described in the opening chapter how culture drives systems design. The Best Practice companies know that culture is a critical factor in designing systems. To be effective, systems must be congruent with the culture. Whether it be nurturing or demeaning, culture is the bedrock of any institution. It is so powerful that any program or system that does not fit within its mores and rituals will not be sustainable.

Customer Focused

Everyone claims to be customer focused today. To admit to anything else is to ostracize yourself from any discussion of effective organizational practices. However, there are two ways to focus on customer needs. The more common is the reactive approach. It is played out in one of two styles. One is simply to wait until someone rings our bell and then we salivate appropriately. In short, when the customer calls, we come running and provide whatever is requested. The other reactive style is to go out to the customer and ask what is desired from our list of products and services. Having checked off the appropriate boxes from column A and column B we then do our best to deliver.

The proactive approach begins by asking the customer a series of questions regarding what the customer is trying to achieve. The focus is on the customer's work and goals, not on the supplier's products. This style operates on the presumption that the customer does not want the supplier's products. What the customer wants is to achieve his or her objectives. This is a not-too-subtle but extremely important difference. After obtaining all pertinent information from the customer, the supplier analyzes the data and attempts to diagnose what types of problems or opportunities the customer has that the supplier might service. Having done this, the supplier returns to the customer and recommends something that will help him or her achieve the objectives.

The proactive method is typical of Best Practice companies. They realize that professionals are hired to diagnose problems and offer solutions. Companies pay for their specialized knowledge and expect them to drive those activities in which they are the specialists.

Interdependence

Best Practice departments realize that the work of one section affects the work of other sections. Most people react to the statement by commenting that it borders on the obvious and that of course their department recognizes the interdependence. Nevertheless, observations in dozens of companies show that actual practice does not support this recognition. If anything, the norm is what I call "feudal management." In feudalism, each local chief (section head) does his or her best to protect the fiefdom from other local chiefs (section heads). In practice, the landscape is strewn with competing baronies.

Best Practice departments are characterized by ongoing formal and informal meetings across the sections to review the effects of one group's work on another group's programs. The value of this constant communication is obvious. Not only do efficiency and effectiveness improve but the personal relationships within the groups are also more positive. Feudalism is replaced with nationalism. In addition, the department presents a consistent image to the rest of the organization that inspires confidence and engenders a heightened spirit of cooperation.

Never Satisfied

Some people are happy when they win more than they lose. Others are only content when they are in the top ranks. Best Practice types are never satisfied . . . period!

The human resources professionals in the study were operating in the top ranks of the twenty-fifth percentile. In fact, most were in about the ninety-sixth percentile. Yet, none of them were satisfied with their results. This does not mean that they are disheartened. On the contrary, they are quite proud of what they have achieved—but they are not about to rest, even at this level.

Repeatedly, after describing what had happened to cause the exceptional results they had obtained, they immediately stated that they had an idea or a plan to make it better. In some cases they were self-deprecating. While acknowledging our congratulations on their accomplishments, they told us how they intended to improve next year. Benchmarking projects have shown us that the best groups in any function are always trying to improve. Other people feel good when they improve performance a notch or two. Then, they stop to rest and celebrate. In the meantime, the best are still working on being even better. And the gap continues to widen. If there were a single personal trait that separated the best from the rest, this never-satisfied attitude would be in the forefront of contenders.

Relationships

When we look back over the successes that the Best Practice groups have had, inevitably we find that the human element is a key issue. Everyone who has ever been part of an organization knows that nothing of real value gets done without the support of the people who work there. Although employees and managers can be coerced to support a program out of fear of losing their jobs, no long-term improvements can be made or sustained without the active support of everyone from the lowest to the highest. It is virtually impossible to install and maintain an effective program when the key people are not involved and committed to making it work.

The Best Practice people described over and over how they had enlisted the support of influential individuals in their organizations. They acknowledged that all the technical knowledge in the world would not have made a difference until strategic alliances had been created. The secret to success was the relationships they built up and traded on when necessary. People in pivotal positions were approached before a major change was attempted. The project was described to them. The potential value of the changes was outlined and the downside of not doing it was explained. Only after the relationships were established did the Best Practice people act. Without key supporters, success is highly unlikely.

In contrast, we have known many competent, even technically brilliant and intellectually superior managers and professionals who have been unable to put their programs through because they did not know how to stimulate imaginations and build consensus. Their careers often have the pattern of one initial success followed by frustration and wandering from company to company, job to job, because they are incapable of building relationships. Indeed, in many cases they were afraid to attempt it.

A manager's success rests on helping his or her staff learn how to acquire and exercise the skills required to build relationships with peers and superiors. No manager can be successful without this capability.

Risk Taking

The Best Practice people seem to be fearless. In some cases they appear downright foolhardy. A second look, however, reveals that they know when to take risks and they are not afraid to try them.

This study confirmed our previous observations of exceptional performance. Often the best performers will take risks that would frighten the devil. We have seen departments totally restructured starting at the level of job descriptions and functional titles. One department director threw out all past structure and traditional function titles and reformed the group as a business. The new functional titles corresponded to standard business structures: R&D, production, marketing, customer service, and administration. The old foundation had to be removed so that people could not hide in it. It was a classic example of structure driving behavior. Without the old structure, new behavior was the only course. If the change had backfired, the director would have been on the street. It was a shocking move, but it worked. In reality, it was the only chance he had for generating real change.

One of the most threatening risks to many staff people is to drop a service. Until the dynamics of the new marketplace changed the rules of organization, staff managers were rewarded for building the largest staffs and budgets possible. They did this by continually taking on more projects, programs, and services. This expansion justified larger staffs and budgets which, in turn, justified higher levels of authority and more money.

Now the rules have changed. Cost control, downsizing, and outsourcing are the new concepts of management. Paradoxically, while many staff managers complain that they don't have enough resources, they are reluctant to stop providing something because they still operate under the old model. This is not true with the Best Practice people. In several instances they conducted customer service surveys that went beyond asking how satisfied the customers were. These surveys generated information on the perceived need the customers had for a given service and showed that there were products, services, or reports that no one really wanted. Thus, they were able to discontinue the service and reallocate their resources to something more valuable. This is another example of how to make what seems to be a risky move without actually taking much risk.

Strategy and Planning

The Best Practice people do what the management theorists prescribe. They actually work from a strategy and they prepare plans that they adhere to. Despite the volatility of today's marketplace, which can severely disrupt the best plans, these professionals are able to operate from a consistent strategy. It seems impossible for anyone to work from a strategic plan these days when the forces driving the plan change before the document comes off the press. The evidence and testimony suggest that those who have the unusual capability to do so are guided by a well-considered, clearly articulated, and thoroughly disseminated vision of their department's function within the enterprise.

With the vision as the lodestar, strategies are developed to support its aims and objectives. From the strategies flow superordinate goals, operating plans, time-bound objectives, and ultimately, specific related actions. As unforeseen change makes its impact on the group, it is relatively easy to shift a resource or change a direction to respond effectively to the new force and serve the always visible, fully understood role.

Strategy to these people does not mean a dust-covered tome on someone's shelf. Their strategies do not revolve around programs. Strategies are roles, relationships, and contributions to corporate imperatives. They go well beyond identifying gaps between future corporate needs and future available resources. Strategy is an aspect of culture. It is a way of life. When the market changes, inside or outside the organization, they can shift to meet the changes without disrupting everything that was previously planned. Strategy is not an exercise; it is organic.

Conclusion

A benchmarking project must start with clear definitions and objectives. In the project reported in this chapter, the key was to select only those companies that had objective data supporting the effectiveness of their processes. This step established the validity of our decision to include them among the best. Popularity or publicity had nothing to do with selection. Several of the companies profiled arc not known outside their immediate community.

After validating a result as deserving to be included among the best, the next question has to do with how the outcomes were achieved. What it by luck or design? This step is more difficult because to answer the question we need to find correlations between the activity and the results. How can we say that the outcome was achieved by something other than luck? Since this is not a laboratory where all variables can be manipulated, we cannot expect to exercise control over the organization or the marketplace. Therefore, proof is not the point. We have to settle for reasonable inferential data. These are obtained by thorough questioning that relates the process to the outcome. In this case, the outcome is backed up with quantitative support.

The great lesson of this project was that the secret of best performance was not to be found in *what* was done. Its genesis was in *why* it was done and why it was done that particular way. The conclusion was that driving forces based on corporate and personal values, strategies, and traits dictated what was done and how it would be done. This line of reasoning goes back to vision. Vision describes who we are and why we are here. Once that is clear, authentic value-adding activities can be undertaken with some assurance that we are doing the best thing.

Epilogue

In my last book, *Human Value Management* (Fitz-enz, 1991), I pointed out that the world is experiencing evolutionary change at revolutionary speed. This massive amount of change coming from all quarters at velocities that we have never before experienced is creating in us a chaotic state of mind. But remember that chaos is nothing more than a pattern we don't recognize. Once we comprehend what is happening to the world market, we will no longer see it as chaotic. The first nations and business enterprises that recognize the new pattern will be the ones that return to prosperity first.

We are also seeing the natural law of reciprocity at work. During the 1950s and 1960s, the pendulum of prosperity in the United States swung to an all-time high. In the early 1970s it paused as other nations came more strongly into the world markets. By the late 1970s and through the 1980s the pendulum began its inexorable swing back from prosperity to economic hardship. The apparent affluence of the early 1980s was a mirage. We ignored basic principles of wealth building—that is, adding value—and now we are paying for it. It seems that the cycle is about to reach its nadir. The natural law of reciprocity states that it should start to swing back toward prosperity, but we need to help the cycle reverse itself.

When economic circumstances become desperate, as they certainly are today, we need to reexamine the fundamentals of wealth creation and maintenance. My observation, based on more than thirty years in business, is that there are three basic building blocks of a commercial enterprise:

- Having a clear purpose
- Understanding the customer's true needs
- Building the capability to serve your purpose and your customer

To me, all three of these hinge on one word: value. General Electric chief executive Jack Welch tells us that the 1990s are the Value Decade (Fortune, 1993):

> The Value Decade has already begun, with global price competition like you've never seen . . . there's an enormous drive to get value, value, value. It doesn't matter where you are anymore because distribution systems now give everybody access to everything.
> The world is moving too fast. What should a company do? First of all, define its vision and its destiny in broad but clear terms. Second, maximize its own productivity. Finally, be organizationally and culturally flexible enough to meet massive change. Be the highest value supplier in your marketplace. You need an overarching message, something big but simple and understandable.

For me, no message is as simple and understandable as this: create value! If you are to create value in your work environment, start by reexamining the purpose of your organization or business unit. Do your people have a clear vision of value? Do they see how that vision plays out in your products and in the market? Reconsider your internal and external performance drivers. Are they adding to or detracting from value? Then, review what your customers need. This is where benchmarking comes in. It starts with value planning, which is based on customers' needs. What is most important to them: price, timeliness, quality, availability, or some human factor? It is probably a combination of two or more. Does your product give your customer status, security, convenience, and/or some other value? Are the values changing? Companies who fail to recognize changing customer values usually suffer severe loss of market share.

Finally, audit your operation. Are you capable of serving competitively your customers' most important values? Benchmarking comes in here also. How are the best people performing the value-adding task required by your customer? Let me caution you at this point not to focus solely on the process, the *what*. The real best practice is a result of *why* and *how*. As I mentioned in Chapter Nine, we discovered that best practice is a function of values, strategies, and interactions rather than of activities.

In the mid 1980s I noticed the same phenomenon during a research project on white-collar worker effectiveness. I reported in the American Management Association's May/June 1986 issue of *Management Review* that worker effectiveness was driven by certain underlying or basic management principles (Fitz-enz, 1986a, 1986b). It was not a function of the latest management magic wand.

Reengineering an organization takes time, but if you plan to be around more than a couple of years, it is the only choice you have. We must rebuild our foundations or the next economic ill wind will topple our prosperity again. The downside of rebuilding basics is that it takes time. Total quality management (TQM) programs take at least three years before substantial improvements begin to emerge. It may take five years or more for TQM to become a way of running the business. The problem is that people seem to think they don't have the time to rebuild, so they keep nailing two-by-fours to the sides of rickety corporate structures. It doesn't work. Of course, we have to perform while we are rebuilding. Benchmarking can help here. When benchmarking is applied to building long-term value through improvements that service the customer's needs, you satisfy all three building blocks of organizational success. With these blocks as our foundation, we will create a structure that is solid and sustainable — guided by a clear vision, knowledgeable of customer needs, and committed to value in all our undertakings.

References

Camp, R. C. *Benchmarking: The Search for Industry Best Practices That Lead to Superior Performance.* Milwaukee, Wisc.: American Society for Quality Control Press, 1989.

Crosby, P. B. *Quality Without Tears.* New York: McGraw-Hill, 1984.

Davis, S., and Davidson, B. *20/20 Vision.* New York: Simon & Schuster, 1991.

Deming, W. E. *Out of the Crisis.* Cambridge, Mass.: MIT CAES, 1986.

Fitz-enz, J. *How to Measure Human Resources Management.* New York: McGraw-Hill, 1984.

Fitz-enz, J. "White Collar Productivity, Part One: The Employee's Side." *Management Review,* May 1986, pp. 52–54.

Fitz-enz, J. "White Collar Effectiveness, Part Two: The Organization's Side." *Management Review,* June 1986, pp. 52–56.

Fitz-enz, J. *Human Value Management: The Value-Adding Human Resource Management Strategy for the 1990s.* San Francisco: Jossey-Bass, 1991.

Foley, P., and Howes, P. *International Best Practices Report on Human Resource Management.* Brisbane, Australia: HRM Consulting Pty. Ltd., 1992.

Fortune magazine, Jan. 25, 1993.

Harrington, J. J. *Business Process Improvement.* New York: McGraw-Hill, 1991.

Juran, J. M. *Juran on Planning for Quality.* New York: Free Press, 1988.

Kami, M. J. *Trigger Points.* New York: McGraw-Hill, 1988.

Kanter, R. M. *The Change Masters.* New York: Simon & Schuster, 1983.

Leibfried, K., and McNair, C. *Benchmarking: A Tool for Continuous Improvement.* New York: HarperCollins, 1992.

Mager, R. F., and Pipe, P. *Analyzing Performance Problems.* Belmont, Calif.: Fearon-Janus, 1970.

Saratoga Institute. *Best Practices Report—1992.* Saratoga, Calif.: Saratoga Institute, 1992.

Schein, E. H. *Process Consultation: Its Role in Organization Development.* Redding, Mass.: Addison-Wesley, 1969.

Senge, P. M. *The Fifth Discipline.* New York: Doubleday, 1990.

Sloma, R. S. *How to Measure Managerial Performance.* New York: Macmillan, 1980.

Society for Human Resource Management (SHRM) and Saratoga Institute (SI). *U.S. Human Resources Effectiveness Report.* Saratoga, Calif.: SHRM/SI, 1991.

Spendolini, M. J. *The Benchmarking Book.* New York: AMACOM, 1992.

Index

A

Accounts receivable, benchmarking for, 86–87, 98–99

Action: approaches for, 150–171; communication in, 150–152; conclusion on, 169–171; and driving toward goal, 164–166; and planning for change, 167–169; and report preparation, 152–157; and report structures, 157–164

Activities: avoid trap of, 26–54; and value planning, 76–77, 78–79

Airlines, and customer values, 10–11

Alcoa, benchmarking by, 39

Amdahl, as partner, 182

American Management Association, 83, 209

American Productivity and Quality Center, 83, 91, 137, 173

American Society for Personnel Administration, 190

American Society for Quality Control, 83, 137

Asset management, and measurement, 57–59

AT&T, benchmarking at, 50

Australia, managing large project in, 181–186

Automobile industry, and values, 9–10, 22

B

Ball Seed Company, sales computers at, 69

Bank One, as partner, 182

Baxter, as partner, 182

Benchmarking: action for change in, 150–171; activities and outcomes

for, 84; and adding value, 4, 12–15, 19–23; basic principles for, 26–54; benefits of, 41–42; and best practices, 187–206; conclusion on, 53–54; data development for, 101–127; defining, 26–28; diagnoses for, 14–15; distinctions of, 29–32; efficient, 76–79; evaluating performance gaps in, 128–149; expectations of, 33–38; forms of, 30–31, 50; hallmarks of, 27–38; managing large-scale, 172–186; measurement in, 55–57; menu of, 27–28; mistakes in, 38; practicing, 91; process of, 3–4, 26, 29, 51; reasons for, 39–41; roles in, 88–90; for special purposes, 41; for staff departments, 4–8; as tool, 32–33; value model of, 50–52; value planning for, 74–100
Best practices: assessing, 187–206; benchmarks for, 190–193; conclusion on, 205–206; defining, 188–190; findings on, 194–195; and gap analysis, 196–197; group profile for, 193; revenue and profitability in, 195–196; sources of, 197–205
Boeing, benchmarking at, 26–27
British Airways, and culture, 16
Bureau of National Affairs, 137

C

California, biotech partners in, 49
Camp, R. C., 27, 50
Change: commitment to, 150–171; concept of, 167; planning for, 142–147, 167–169; resistance to, 141–142, 144–146; sources of, 168; tactics for, 144–146; and value added, 146–147
Colgate, as partner, 182
Comalco Minerals and Alumina, 181
Commerce Clearing House, 137
Commitment: in best practices, 198–199; expectation of, 35–36
Communication: in best practices,

199; imperatives for, 151–152; opportunities for, 152; with reports, 152–164
Competitive analysis, benchmarking distinct from, 29
Competitive partners, sources of, 46–47
Connecticut Mutual Life, as partner, 182
Connections, expectations of, 36
Consultants, for large projects, 176
Continuous improvement, and performance gaps, 130, 142–143, 149
Critical success factors, and value planning, 76
Crosby, P. B., 136
Culture: in best practices, 199–200; in value-adding chain, 15–16
Customers: in best practices, 200–201; concept of, 19–20; losing touch with, 22–23; needs of, 13–14, 52; value to, 10–12

D

Data development: approaches for, 101–127; from benchmarking, 41–42; checklist for, 127; for closing gaps, 128; collection method for, 111–119; conclusion on, 124–127; ethical issues in, 120–121; at home company, 102–103; issues in, 111–113; in managing large projects, 178–179, 182–183; and misdirection, 134–135; organizations and analysis for, 121–124, 135–137; problems with, 132–134; project portfolio for, 119–120; questionnaire design for, 103–111
Davidson, B., 147
Davis, S., 147
Defensiveness, and partners, 49
Deming, W. E., 56, 136
Digital Equipment Company (DEC), benchmarking at, 26–27, 50
Dissatisfaction, in best practices, 201–202
Drucker, P., 56

E

Edison Electric Institute, 172
Electric Power Research Institute, 83
Electronics industry: managing large project for, 174–181; performance drivers of, 94
Employees, value for, 9–10
Ethical issues, in data development, 120–121
Evaluation, for closing performance gaps, 128–149
Evidence, from benchmarking, 42

F

Federal Express: benchmarking at, 50; and halo effect, 92; as partner, 182
Financial values, concept of, 21
Findings, in reports, 159, 162
First Tennessee Bank, as partner, 182
Fitz-enz, J., 83, 144, 194, 207, 209
Florida Power and Light, benchmarking at, 50
Focus groups, for data collection, 117

G

Galvin, B., 17, 130
Gaps, performance: approaches for closing, 128–149; and best practices, 196–197; change strategy for, 142–147; conclusion on, 147–149; interpreting, 132–139; locating, 131–132; performance drivers of, 132–137; projecting and calculating, 139–142; steps in evaluating, 128–130; "why" questions for, 137–139
General Electric, and value, 208
General Motors, and customer values, 22
Generic partners, sources of, 48–49
GMAC Mortgage, as partner, 182
Goals, in action phase, 165–166

H

Harrington, J. J., 136
Hewlett-Packard, time for closing gap at, 148
Hino Motors, delivery time at, 147
HRM Consulting of Brisbane, 181, 183
Human Resources Benchwork Network, 173
Human values: concept of, 21; in reports, 164

I

Icahn, C., 11
Imitation, expectation for, 34
Impacts, measurement of, 68–69
Institutionalization, for change, 143, 168–169
Integration, expectations of, 36–37
Intel, as partner, 182
Interdependence, in best practices, 201
Internal partners, sources of, 44–46
International Business Machines (IBM): benchmarking at, 50; culture of, 94; and Workforce Solutions, 22–23
Interview, format for, 184–185

J

Japan: commitment in, 198; delivery time in, 147; employees as owners in, 10; imitation of, 34, 138; reverse engineering in, 114; value in, 20
Juran, J. M., 136

K

Kami, M. J., 157
Kanter, R. M., 167
Kearns, D., 26, 42
Kobe, competition with, 39

L

Labor unions, and value failures, 10
Large projects. *See* Managing large projects

Learning, expectation of, 35
Leverage, reverse, 5-6
Leibfried, K., 50, 60, 83
L. L. Bean, and halo effect, 92

M

McNair, C., 50, 60, 83
Majer, R. F., 135
Malcolm Baldrige National Quality
    Award, 24
Managing large projects: approaches
    for, 172-186; in Australia,
    181-186; conclusion on, 186;
    data development in, 178-179,
    182-183; for electronics com-
    pany, 174-181; issues and princi-
    ples in, 173-175; partner selec-
    tion in, 177-178, 182; process
    control in, 173; reports in,
    179-180, 183-185; scope setting
    in, 176-177, 181-182
Marshall, C., 16
MCI Communications, as partner,
    182
Measurement: applications of,
    55-73; and asset management,
    57-59; in benchmarking, 55-57;
    benchmarking distinct from, 30;
    conclusion on, 72-73; expecta-
    tions of, 37-38; of impacts,
    68-69; neglect of, 56-57; or-
    ganic, 59-61; of outcomes,
    66-68; of processes, 63-66;
    resistance to, 62-63, 64-65, 67;
    and value chain, 63-72; and
    value creation, 21-22, 61-62,
    69-72
Mellon Bank, as partner, 182
Memorial Sloan-Kettering Cancer
    Center, as partner, 182
Methods, in reports, 160-161,
    162-163
Motorola: benchmarking at, 26-27;
    customers and clients at, 20; and
    halo effect, 92; participative man-
    agement at, 130; as partner, 182;
    and performance, 17; six sigma
    target of, 140-141

N

National Aeronautics and Space Ad-
    ministration (NASA), 139-140
National Australia Bank, 181
Networks: for benchmarking teams,
    91; and managing large projects,
    173; and reports, 156-157
Noncompetitive partners, sources of,
    47-48

O

O'Neill, P., 39
Operations and administration level,
    benchmarking for, 40-41
Organizations: organic measurement
    of, 59-61; reengineering,
    209-210
Outcomes: measurement of, 66-68;
    and value planning, 76-77, 79
Outsourcing, impact of, 22-23

P

Pacific Gas and Electric, as partner,
    182
Participation, for change, 142, 169
Partners: from benchmarking, 42;
    characteristics of, 45; contacting,
    95-97, 99; criteria for selecting,
    92-93; data development with,
    101-127; for large projects,
    177-178, 182; sources of, 43-49,
    92
Performance: gaps in, 128-149;
    measurement of, 55-73; in value-
    adding chain, 17
Performance drivers: checklist of,
    133; concept of, 15; of gaps,
    132-137; and value planning,
    93-95
Personal contact, for data collection,
    115-119
Peters, T., 56
Pipe, P., 135
Planning: strategic, 40, 204-205;
    value, 74-100
Pogo, 24

Process area, and value planning, 76–78

Process owner role, 88–89

Processes, measurement of, 63–66

Production values, concept of, 20–21

Project leader role, 89

Project portfolio, for data development, 119–120

Project team: recruiting, 87–91, 99, 100; relationships for, 91; role of, 89; skill building for, 90

Purpose, in reports, 158–159, 161–162

Q

Quality, value distinct from, 19

Questionnaire: for data development, 103–111; organization and layout of, 106–108; testing for clarity of, 108–109

Questions: application of, 109–111; for best practices, 192; content of, 105–106; number of, 104–105; structure of, 103–104

R

Recommendations, in reports, 159–160, 163

Relationships, in best practices, 202–203

Reports: audience for, 153–155; executive summary of, 158–161; formats for, 155–157; guidelines for, 157–158; human factor in, 164; in large projects, 179–180, 183–185; main, 161–164; preparing, 152–157; purpose of, 164; structuring, 157–164

Research, for data collection, 113–115

Results, in value-adding chain, 17–18

Reverse engineering, for data collection, 114–115

Risk taking, in best practices, 203–204

Rohm and Haas, as partner, 182

Round table: for data collection, 119; for large projects, 179

S

Sample Company: action phase at, 170–171; data management by, 125; evaluation of gaps by, 148; value planning by, 98–99

Saratoga Institute: and action phase, 162; and benchmarking, 33, 35, 42, 50; and best practices project, 187–206; and data development, 122–123; and managing large projects, 173, 174, 181, 182; and measurement, 55, 60, 64, 69; and performance gaps, 135, 137; and value, 4, 6n, 7n; and value planning, 75, 82, 83, 91, 96; vision for, 85–86, 165

Schein, E. H., 135

Schulz, U., 19, 66

Senge, P. M., 35

"Should be" syndrome, 33–34

Site visits, for data collection, 117–118

Sloma, R. S., 83

Society for Human Resource Management (SHRM), 181, 182, 189, 190, 191

Spendolini, M. J., 27, 28n, , 50

Staff departments: adding value to, 1–25; benchmarking for, 4–8; customers of, 22; leverage by, 5–6; measures for, 61; value created by, 5, 82

Stakeholders: as audience for reports, 153; for process, 89

Strategic planning: and benchmarking, 40; in best practices, 204–205

Strategic Planning Institute, 83, 91

Support staff, role of, 89

Surveying, benchmarking distinct from, 29–30

Surveys, for data collection, 116–117

Systems, in value-adding chain, 16–17

T

Target function, and value planning, 76–77
Teamwork: from benchmarking, 41; in project, 87–91, 99, 100
Telephone interviews, for data collection, 115–116
3M Company: and halo effect, 92; and performance drivers, 15
Total quality management (TQM): and benchmarking, 39–40; time lapse for, 209–210
TWA, customer service lacking at, 11
Typically Ltd. Company: action phase at, 154, 166; connections at, 36; data development at, 109; measurement at, 63; performance gaps at, 129, 131–132, 134–135, 146; staff problems at, 1–3, 18, 23; value planning at, 75, 76, 79

U

Unfreezing and refreezing, in change process, 167–169
U.S. Chamber of Commerce, 137

V

Value: building blocks for, 21–23; centrality of, 208; conclusion on, 24–25; customer definitions of, 11–12; decade of, 208; defining, 74; for employees, 9–10; loss of, 23; potential, 65–66; quality distinct from, 19; types of, 20–21; vision of, 8–15
Value adding: approaches for, 1–25; and benchmarking, 4, 12–15, 19–23; centrality of, 1, 207–210; and change, 146–147; and measuring, 21–22, 61–62, 69–72; in value-adding chain, 18

Value-adding chain: and integration, 37; and measurement, 63–72; and vision, 15–18
Value outcomes, and value planning, 76–77, 79
Value path, staff-line customer, 7–8
Value planning: activities in, 74–75, 80–93; applications of, 74–100; and benchmarking, 51–52; comparing value potential in, 83–84, 98; conclusion on, 99–100; contacting partners in, 95–97; and efficiency, 76–79; forming benchmarking team in, 87–91, 99; identifying opportunities in, 80–82, 98; identifying value in, 79–80; locating partners in, 91–93, 99, 100; and performance drivers, 93–95; selecting targets in, 85–87, 98; and structure, 100
Vision: in action phase, 164–166; of value, 8–15; and value-adding chain, 15–18; value creation for, 1–25

W

Wagner, progress at, 19
Washington, Researchers, 83
Watson, T., 94
Welch, J., 208
Whirlpool, as partner, 182
Wilson, C., 22

X

Xerox: benchmarking at, 26, 27, 42, 50; and halo effect, 92

Y

Young, J., 148

Z

"Z" Chart, 31